Book D

Elementary Language Skills

Grammar, Usage, and Mechanics of Writing

Phoenix Learning Resources, LLC.

Educational Consultants

Juan Flores, Dallas Independent School District, Dallas Texas

James Giachino, formerly of Rumson Public Schools, Rumson, New Jersey

Harriet Walker, Ladue Public Schools, St, Louis County, Missouri

Phoenix Learning Resources, LLC.
914 Church Street • Honesdale, PA 18431
1-800-228-9345 • Fax: 570-253-3227 • www.phoenixlr.com

Item# 1285   ISBN 978-0-7915-1285-2

TABLE OF CONTENTS

1 Singular and Plural Nouns

Try It

Circle three nouns in the sentence. Write them on the lines.

The girl and her family camped in the mountains.

_____ _____ _____

☐ First Check: Did you circle *girl, family,* and *mountains* ?

RULE: Nouns name people, animals, places, or things.

girl	mountains	bear
boy	flatlands	dinner

Circle three nouns in each sentence.

1. In the morning, the girl runs through the forest.
2. The sky is deep blue, the lake shines brightly, and the evergreens are, of course, green.
3. Large gray stones and rotting logs dot the hillside.
4. A brook gurgles nearby; the water gleams in the sunlight.
5. After taking off her shoes and rolling up her pants, she wades in the icy stream.
6. The harsh call of a bluejay breaks the silence.
7. A bear with a large black head is wandering down the path.

RULE: A singular noun names one person, place, or thing. A plural noun names more than one.

mountain—mountains   bear—bears

Add _s_ to most nouns to make them plural. Add _es_, to singular nouns that end in _s, x, ch,_ or _sh_.

guess—guesses   box—boxes

Fix It

Write the plural form of each underlined noun.

8. The bear left the path and was hidden by the tall <u>grass</u>.
9. "He must catch fish for his <u>lunch</u>," the young girl thought.
10. Suddenly she heard <u>noise</u> at the camp.
11. It sounded like breaking <u>dish</u>.
12. Someone was throwing <u>box</u> around, too.
13. She heard her mother shout, "He's eating the <u>sandwich</u>!"

4

8. _____ 10. _____ 12. _____

9. _____ 11. _____ 13. _____

Add the correct plural ending for each noun.

14. mountain _____   17. fire _____   20. ax _____

15. guess _____   18. bird _____   21. birch _____

16. tax _____   19. ash _____   22. cabin _____

> **RULE:** **Some words have irregular plural forms. The spelling of these words changes when they become plural.**
>
> foot—feet   tooth—teeth   mouse—mice
> man—men   child—children   goose—geese
>
> **Some words do not change in the plural.**
>
> moose—moose   deer—deer

Fix It

Circle the incorrect plural noun in each sentence and write it correctly on the line.

23. The girl ran to the camp as fast as her foots would carry her.
24. The campers were hiding behind a tree as quiet as mouses.
25. The only sound was the chattering of her brother's tooths.
26. The bear didn't notice the childs or the adults.
27. After a while the bear lumbered off, making as much noise as a herd of mooses.
28. "We look like a bunch of silly gooses," the girl said, "but what can you do when an 800-pound bear walks into your camp?"

23. _____ 25. _____ 27. _____

24. _____ 26. _____ 28. _____

Write It

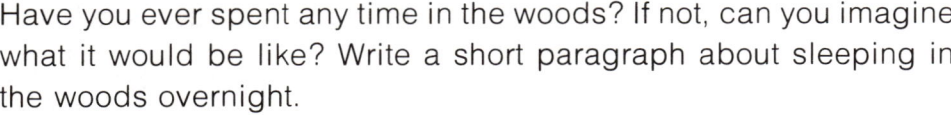

Have you ever spent any time in the woods? If not, can you imagine what it would be like? Write a short paragraph about sleeping in the woods overnight.

Try It

Circle one common noun and underline one proper noun in this sentence.

My favorite book came from Dublin, Ireland.

☐ First Check: Did you circle *book*? Did you underline *Dublin, Ireland*?

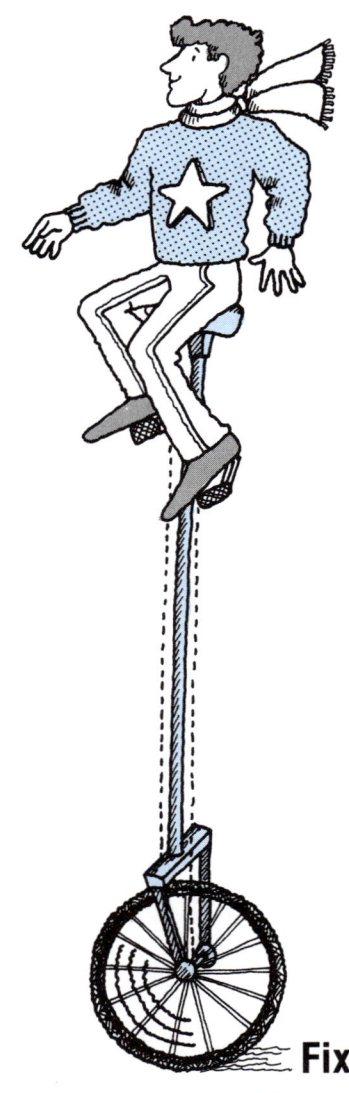

> **RULE:** **Words that name classes of people, places, and things are *common nouns*. Words that name particular people, places, or things are *proper nouns*. *Proper nouns* begin with capital letters.**
>
> | Common Nouns | Proper Nouns |
> |---|---|
> | person | Henri Rochetain |
> | country | France |
> | magazine | Newsweek |

Here are some strange travel facts from the *Guinness Book of World Records*. Underline the proper nouns in each sentence. Circle the common nouns in each sentence.

1. Henri Rochetain walked 3,411 m (3,790 yards) on a tightrope.
2. He did this in almost four hours at Clermont-Ferand, France.
3. Abilene, Texas, was the home of Plennie L. Wingo.
4. He walked backwards from Fort Worth, Texas, to Istanbul, Turkey. It took almost two years.
5. In 1967 Clinton Shaw started out from Victoria, British Columbia.
6. He roller-skated for 7,840 km (4,900 miles) on the Trans-Canadian Highway.
7. Shaw reached Newfoundland in six and a half months.

Fix It

Circle the one mistake in each sentence. Then write the noun correctly on the line.

8. In 1970 Sally Younger traveled 169 km/h (105.14 miles per hour) on Water skis.
9. Steve McPeak traveled 3,218 km (2,000 miles) from chicago.
10. He made the trip to las vegas on a unicycle that was 3.9 m (13 feet) tall.
11. One day in 1974 Lt. col. Richard Cranshaw went for a walk.

12. The man from liverpool did not stop for 72 hours and 54 minutes.
13. R. Cranshaw had clocked over two hundred thirty-one Miles (372 km).
14. Lyn Cox was only 16 years old on august 10, 1973, when she took a famous swim.
15. In 9 hours and 36 minutes she swam 34 km (21 miles) across the english Channel.

8. _____   12. _____

9. _____   13. _____

10. _____   14. _____

11. _____   15. _____

Use It

The pronouns *I* and *me* are often confused. The pronoun *I* is used as the subject of a sentence.

I want to set a record.   Frannie and *I* will walk home.

The pronoun *me* is used after verbs. It is also used after words like *to, from, by*, and *with*.

Will you walk with *me*?   Marie will time *me*.

Complete each sentence. Write *I* or *me* on the line.

16. "_____ want to be in the *Guinness Book of World Records*."

17. "Are you kidding _____?"

18. "World records don't scare _____ at all."

19. "First _____ have to find a sport with no records."

20. "My teacher and _____ can hop nonstop for four minutes."

21. "Tell _____, will that be good enough?"

Write It

If you could set a record, what would it be? Tell how you would feel immediately after you set this record. Use several proper nouns in your paragraph.

3   Abbreviations

Try It   Circle the abbreviations in this sentence.

Dr. Thorne parked her car on Atlantic Ave. at 4 P.M.

☐   First Check: Did you circle *Dr., Ave.,* and **P.M.**?

> **RULE: An abbreviation is a shortened form of a word. Most abbreviations end with periods.**
>
> Mister—Mr.   Ante Meridiem—A.M.   pounds—lbs.
> boulevard—blvd.   October—Oct.   New York—N.Y.

Write these abbreviations next to the words they stand for: km, tsp., hdqrs., doz., Rd., P.S., St., Inc., mm, Blvd., Co., Jr., hr., P.M., Sr., Dr.

1. Boulevard _____

2. Street _____

3. headquarters _____

4. kilometer _____

5. hour _____

6. Junior _____

7. Postscript _____

8. millimeter _____

9. Incorporated _____

10. Post Meridiem _____

11. Road _____

12. dozen _____

13. teaspoon _____

14. Company _____

15. Senior _____

16. Doctor _____

> **RULE: The names of groups and organizations are *proper nouns*. These names can be abbreviated by using the first letter of each word. Small words like *and, of*, and *the* are not usually included in an abbreviation.**
>
> Federal Bureau of Investigation—F.B.I.   United Nations—U.N.

Write an abbreviation for each proper noun.

17. American Kennel Club
18. American Broadcasting Company
19. Environmental Protection Agency
20. Food and Drug Administration

17. _____   18. _____

19. _____   20. _____

8

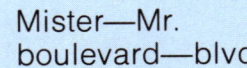

Circle the abbreviation in each sentence. Write the word or words it stands for on the line.

21. Amy and her mother drove to Sycamore St. in Central City.
22. They parked behind the Telephone Co. building.
23. The animal shelter was at the corner of Myrtle Ave.
24. Amy laughed; a man named Dr. Katz ran the place.
25. Amy chose a sheep dog. It was registered with the A.K.C.
26. The dog weighed about 9 kg (20 lbs.).
27. She named the dog Sam Thorne Sr. because it was hard to say.
28. The doctor said Sam was 1 m tall.
29. Sam had been a sheep dog in upstate N.Y.

21. _____   24. _____   27. _____

22. _____   25. _____   28. _____

23. _____   26. _____   29. _____

On the lines, write one word in each sentence as an abbreviation.

30. Amy and her mother drove to their home in Monroe County.
31. Dr. Thorne works for the Environmental Protection Agency.
32. Sam loved wandering on the land that Doctor Thorne owns.
33. One day Sam did not come back for many hours.
34. Finally Amy heard his bark. She looked down Maple Road.
35. Sam was chasing at least one dozen sheep.
36. Amy thought the sheep belonged to Mister Allen.
37. He lived 10 kilometers (6.2 miles) away.
38. "I guess you really are a sheep dog," Amy said, as she called police headquarters.

30. _____   33. _____   36. _____

31. _____   34. _____   37. _____

32. _____   35. _____   38. _____

Write It   Think about some of the abbreviations you see every day. Write a short paragraph that uses at least five abbreviations.

Try It

Write the subject pronoun in this sentence.

She makes bowls in front of her house. _____

☐ First Check: Did you write the pronoun *she*?

> **RULE:** A *pronoun* can be used in place of a noun. *I, you, he, she, it, we*, and *they* are *subject pronouns*. These *pronouns* tell who or what does something in a sentence. The underlined words are subject pronouns.
>
> Michael Gillespie lives with Aunt Felicity in Arizona. <u>He</u> loves his aunt very much. Aunt Felicity is a potter. <u>She</u> makes large blue bowls from clay.

Circle the subject pronoun in each sentence.

1. "Would you like to help me?" Felicity asks.
2. "Yes, I would," Michael answers.
3. "Good, we will work together."
4. She uses clay mixed with water.
5. She shows Michael how to roll the clay into long strips.
6. He tries to roll some clay snakes.
7. They must stick to each other tightly.
8. She winds the strips into circles called coils.
9. As she builds up layers of coils, a bowl takes shape.
10. She puts the bowl in the sun to dry.
11. After drying, it must be baked in an oven.

A pronoun can take the place of a noun. On the line, write the pronoun that can take the place of the underlined noun in each of the following sentences.

12. <u>Felicity</u> leaves the pots to bake in the oven all day.
13. <u>The pots</u> get very hard from the heat of the fire.
14. <u>Michael</u> wants to open the hot oven.
15. Finally <u>Felicity and Michael</u> open the door and let the heat out.
16. <u>Michael</u> sees that the clay has changed from brown to red.
17. <u>The pots</u> are now ready to be painted.

12. _____   15. _____

13. _____   16. _____

14. _____   17. _____

The second sentence in each pair contains an object pronoun. Draw a line under the object pronoun. Then write the name or names that each pronoun replaces on the line.

18. "I must buy paint for the pots," Felicity said. "Come with me, Michael."
19. Felicity buys blue paint. She puts it in a bag.
20. Michael watches doves near the shop. The birds fly above him.
21. Michael would like to make doves. He would like to make them with clay.
22. Felicity sees the doves too. "Can doves be made from clay?" Michael asks her.
23. "They are easy to make, Michael. I will show you at home," Felicity answers.

18. _____   21. _____

19. _____   22. _____

20. _____   23. _____

Write It

Have you ever made anything with clay? Was it an animal or a bowl? What would you like to make with clay? Write about what you would make. Circle each subject pronoun you write. Draw a line under each object pronoun.

5 Possessive Nouns

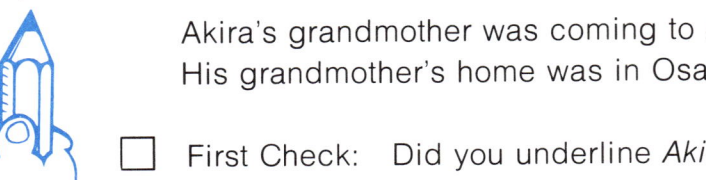

Try It   Underline one word in each sentence that shows possession.

Akira's grandmother was coming to America.
His grandmother's home was in Osaka, Japan.

☐   First Check: Did you underline *Akira's* and *grandmother's*?

> **RULE: Nouns can show ownership or possession. To write the *possessive form* of a singular noun, add an apostrophe (') and *s*. Add only an apostrophe to *plural nouns* and other nouns that end in *s*.**
>
> the grandmother of the boy   the boy's grandmother
> the home of the girls   the girls' home

Rewrite each group of words using a possessive noun.

1. the voice of the speaker   3. the car owned by Dad
2. the hems of the dresses   4. the walls of the rooms

1. _____   3. _____

2. _____   4. _____

Fix It   Circle the word in each sentence that should show ownership or possession. Then write the word with an apostrophe on the lines.

5. Akira walked into the airports waiting room.
6. Travelers voices filled the air.
7. Loudspeakers shouted each planes arriving time.
8. The boy watched as fuel was pumped into one planes tank.

5. _____   7. _____

6. _____   8. _____

Circle the possessive noun in each sentence. If the noun is singular, write *S* on the line. If it is plural, write *P*.

_____ 9. Akira looked through the lobby's windows.
_____ 10. Strangers' faces were staring back.
_____ 11. Akira learned that the airplane's motors are checked every 10,000 miles.

12

_____12. Akira tried to remember Grandmother's face.

_____13. The announcer's voice said the plane from Osaka was landing.

> **RULE:** Some pronouns show ownership. They are called *possessive pronouns*.
>
> | Singular | Plural |
> | --- | --- |
> | my | our |
> | your | your |
> | his, her, its | their |

Choose a possessive pronoun to complete each sentence. Write it on the line.

14. Akira was so excited ____ voice cracked.
15. As passengers walked by, Akira looked carefully at ____ faces.
16. Suddenly he saw Grandmother; ____ face was beaming.
17. "Welcome to America," Akira's mother said. "We hope you will enjoy ____ visit."
18. "We want you to be comfortable. ____ home will be yours."
19. "Where is ____ suitcase, Grandmother?" Akira asked.
20. "The suitcase is green; ____ handle is red," she said.
21. Akira looked everywhere. All the suitcases had been taken by ____ owners.
22. Akira looked again: "Grandmother, ____ suitcase is not there."
23. "They must have left ____ suitcase in Japan," a tall thin man in a red uniform said.
24. Akira could not believe ____ ears.
25. Grandmother laughed; ____ eyes twinkled. "At least they didn't leave me behind," she said.

14. _____	18. _____	22. _____
15. _____	19. _____	23. _____
16. _____	20. _____	24. _____
17. _____	21. _____	25. _____

Write It Write about a trip you would like to take. Tell what you would bring. Use several possessive nouns and pronouns.

6 Writing Pad

Complete the word chart. Fill in each blank in column A with a common noun. Write a proper noun in column B. Write an abbreviation in C, and a possessive noun or pronoun in D.

A Common Noun	B Proper Noun	C Abbreviation	D Possessive Noun or Pronoun
turkey	Arthur	Rd.	father's
1.			
2.			
3.			
4.			

Now write a sentence that uses all four words from each line in the chart. Add as many other words as you need.

Example: Arthur walked with father's turkey on Elderberry Rd.

1. _____

2. _____

3. _____

4. _____

Rewrite each group of words using a possessive noun. Add an apostrophe and s. Now use each possessive noun group in a sentence.

5. the truck belonging to that woman
6. the color of the truck
7. the noise coming from the motor
8. the shouts of the police officers

14

5. _____

_____

6. _____

_____

7. _____

_____

8. _____

_____

9. Write a paragraph that uses at least five of the following pronouns: I, you, he, she, it, we, they, me, him, her, us, them.

_____

_____

_____

_____

USE THE DICTIONARY

A dictionary entry has many parts that tell you about a word.

va•ca•tion (vā kā′ shən) **1** *n.* A period of time for rest or recre-
ation, away from regular work, study, etc. **2** *v.* to take a vacation.

•The entry word is broken into syllables.
•The pronunciation of the word is given in parentheses.
•Many words have more than one meaning. Each different mean-
ing has a different number.
•The entry also tells what part of speech a word is. Sometimes a
word can be used as a noun and a verb.
•The definition of each word is given in the entry.
•This symbol (¯) is a macron. It shows that a vowel is long.
•This is a *schwa* (ə). It is a hard-to-hear vowel.

7 Review

(L 1) Underline the nouns in each sentence.

    1. Manuel was going to visit his sister.
    2. Elena lives in Mexico City.
    3. This city is the capital of the country, Mexico.

(L 1) Underline any singular nouns and circle any plural nouns in each sentence.

    4. Manuel's four brothers packed his bags.
    5. Manuel carried two boxes on the bus to the airport.
    6. His younger sister was sending some special dishes to Elena.
    7. His plane waited on the runway.
    8. They saw other children in the waiting room.

(L 4) Circle the subject pronoun in each sentence.

    9. He said hello to some of them.
   10. They were counting the minutes until their flight.
   11. It was a busy day at the airport.

(L 4) What pronouns could you use as the subjects of these sentences?

   12. A girl said it was ten o'clock.
   13. Manuel thought it was only 9:30.
   14. The children asked a man for the right time.

   12. _____ 13. _____ 14. _____

(L 2) Underline the proper nouns in these sentences.

   15. Manuel boarded the Boeing 747.
   16. Flight Steward Perez gave Manuel a copy of *Time* magazine.
   17. The boy asked for Marvel Comics instead.

(L 2) Circle the proper nouns in the sentences. Then write them correctly on the lines.

   18. His plane took three hours to get to mexico city.
   19. He could not find elena at the airport.

16

20. "Take me to the police chief," he asked officer sanchez.
21. But the officer did not speak english.
22. Then manuel saw his cousin.
23. "We're late," margarita said. "Our car would not start."

18. _____   21. _____

19. _____   22. _____

20. _____   23. _____

(L 3)   Circle the abbreviations in the sentences. Then write them.

24. The city is called Mexico City, d.f., or *Distrito Federal*.
25. It is similar to the way we use D.C. with Washington, District of Columbia.
26. In Spanish, C. stands for Calle and means "street."
27. Avenida is abbreviated Av. and means "avenue."

24. _____   26. _____

25. _____   27. _____

(L 5)   Circle the possessive nouns and pronouns in the sentences. Then write them on the lines.

28. Manuel's sister lives on the C. Mórales.
29. That night Elena took Manuel to the city's big park.
30. Elena packed a picnic in her basket.
31. The park's name was Chapultepec.
32. "That means 'grasshopper hill'," Elena told her brother.
33. The park is Mexico City's playground.
34. Manuel said he would like it to be his park.
35. "It belongs to the people of Mexico City. It is their park."
36. The children smiled and sat on the people's grass.

28. _____   31. _____   34. _____

29. _____   32. _____   35. _____

30. _____   33. _____   36. _____

8 Verb Tenses

Try It

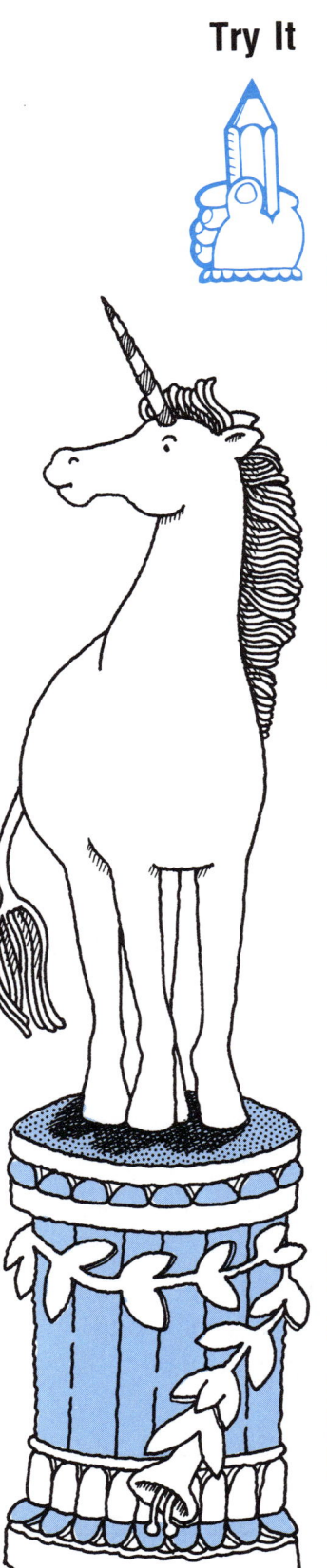

Draw a line under the verb in this sentence. Label the verb *past* or *present* to tell when the action takes place.

Animals and people live side by side. _____

☐ First Check: Did you underline *live* and label it *present*?

> **RULE: A verb is a word that shows action or being. A verb shows time through its different forms. The *present tense* tells what is happening now. It also shows what happens regularly.**
>
> The unicorn, an imaginary animal, *interests* people today.
>
> **The *past tense* of a verb tells what happened in the past. The past tense is often formed by adding *-ed* to the present tense.**
>
> This beast also *interested* people of the Middle Ages.

Draw a line under the verb in each sentence. Decide if it is present or past. Write *present* or *past* on the lines.

1. The unicorn appears in old stories, on paintings, and rugs.
2. The unicorn looked much like a white pony.
3. In pictures its tail looked like a lion's tail.
4. A long horn grew from its head.
5. The white and black horn ended in a red tip.
6. Stories about the unicorn came from ancient Greece.

1. _____   3. _____   5. _____

2. _____   4. _____   6. _____

> **RULE: The *future tense* of a verb tells what will happen in the future. It is formed by using the word *will* before the present tense of the verb.**
>
> The unicorn *will interest* you, too.

Draw a line under the verb or verbs in each sentence. Decide if the verb is *past, present*, or *future*. Write your answers on the lines.

7. Long ago people thought the unicorn was magical.

8. The horn will remove poison from food.
9. In an old picture, the unicorn dips its horn into a stream.
10. This way, the animal makes bad water fresh.
11. People hunted the unicorn for its magical horn.
12. The frightened unicorn can run faster than any horse.

7. _____   9. _____   11. _____

8. _____   10. _____   12. _____

☐   Second Check: Did you underline *will remove* in sentence 8? Did you label it *future*?

Change each verb in the following sentences to the *past tense*. Write the past tense on the line.

13. In one story, men capture the unicorn with a girl's help.
14. The beast walks to the girl.
15. Then the unicorn rests its head in her lap.
16. The young woman pets the unicorn's neck.
17. A servant waves to a man hidden nearby.
18. The man then signals the other hunters to catch the beast.

13. _____   15. _____   17. _____

14. _____   16. _____   18. _____

Change each underlined verb in the following sentences to a verb that shows *future* time. Write your answers on the lines.

19. Everything about the unicorn <u>seems</u> strange to people.
20. Many people <u>think</u> the unicorn was really a rhinoceros.
21. For others the unicorn <u>remains</u> a mystery.
22. Perhaps no one ever <u>understands</u> the unicorn.

19. _____   21. _____

20. _____   22. _____

Write It   Write a short paragraph describing someone's good or bad experiences with a favorite animal character. Use only past tense verbs.

19

9 Irregular Verbs

Try It   Write the past tense of *begin* on the line.

It was the Egyptians who first _____ to keep the cat as a pet.

☐ First Check: Did you write *began*?

> **RULE:** The *past tense* of many verbs is not formed by adding *d* or *ed*. The past tense forms of these irregular verbs have different spellings.
>
> **PRESENT:** bring   eat find   give go   make ring run
> **PAST:**   brought ate found gave went made rang ran

Write the past tense of the irregular verb in each sentence.

1. The ancient Egyptians (give) honor and love to their cats.
2. They (find) the way to tame the cat.
3. Cats solved a big problem because they (eat) rats and mice in Egypt.
4. Harming a cat (bring) punishment to an Egyptian.
5. In a burning house, the Egyptian (runs) to save the cat before anything else.
6. When a cat died, the home (rings) with the sounds of sadness.
7. The dead cat's master (goes) so far as to shave off his eyebrows as a sign of deep feeling.
8. The Egyptians (make) dead cats into mummies.
9. The Egyptians even (have) a cat goddess named Bast.

1. _____   4. _____   7. _____

2. _____   5. _____   8. _____

3. _____   6. _____   9. _____

> **RULE:** *Irregular verbs* change their spelling in the past tense. Often only one vowel in the word changes. Here are more irregular verbs.
>
> **PRESENT:** become blow come do   draw hide know
> **PAST:**   became blew came did drew hid   knew
>
> **PRESENT:** take see sing speak swim wear keep
> **PAST:**   took saw sang spoke swam wore kept

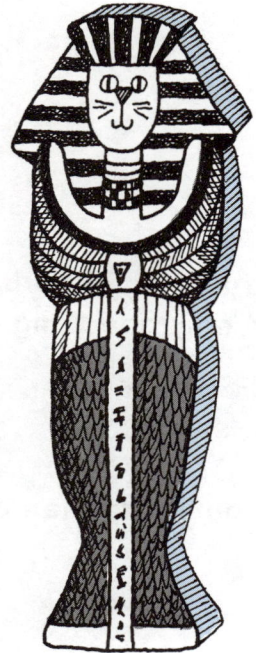

Write the *past tense* of each verb on the lines.

10. When their pet cats died, Egyptians (take) them to a cat cemetery.
11. The Egyptian pet owners (see) to it that mummies of rats and mice, as well as a little dish of milk, were put in each cat's grave.
12. Egyptians (know) that they could die for killing a cat.
13. The Egyptians (make) furniture in the shape of cats.
14. They (wear) cat jewelry.
15. For many, many years the Egyptians (keep) their knowledge of cats a secret.

10. _____   12. _____   14. _____

11. _____   13. _____   15. _____

Fix It

If the underlined verb is in the past tense, write *past* on the line. If the underlined verb is not in the past tense, write the correct past tense on the line.

16. The Egyptians <u>hide</u> this valuable animal from the rest of the world for a long time.
17. In time the Egyptians <u>came</u> to worship their cats as gods.
18. They <u>sing</u> praises to the goddess Bast, who had a cat's head.
19. Egyptians <u>speak</u> of Bast as their guard against sickness.
20. This was probably because they <u>know</u> the cat was a very clean animal.
21. In time the prized cat <u>becomes</u> a favorite animal in Rome and other places, too.

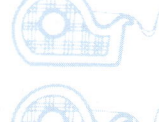

16. _____   18. _____   20. _____

17. _____   19. _____   21. _____

Write It

It is sometimes said that people either love or hate cats. Explain how you have felt about cats in the past. Use only past tense verbs in your paragraph.

21

10 The Verbs Be and Have

Try It

Draw a line under the correct form of the verb *be*.

Dolphins (is/are) interesting animals.

☐ First Check: Did you underline *are*?

> **RULE: The verb *be* has more forms than any other verb. Use *is* or *was* when you talk about only one thing.**
>
> The bottlenose dolphin *is* about 2.6 m (8.5 feet) long.
> The dolphin *was* always a favorite among sailors.
>
> **Use *are* or *were* when you talk about more than one thing.**
>
> Dolphins *are* smaller than whales.
> Dolphins *were* not studied until the 1900s.
>
> **Use *am* and *was* when you talk about yourself.**
>
> I *am* interested in dolphins.   I *was* interested years ago.
>
> **Use *are* and *were* when speaking to someone else.**
>
> If you *were* not sure of the dolphin's talents before, you *are* in for a surprise now.

Draw a line under the correct form of the verb.

1. The dolphin (is, are) a wild animal.
2. Yet dolphins (is, are) different from other wild animals in one important way.
3. You (is, are) probably aware that dolphins (is, are) seen swimming alongside boats and ships.
4. When they do this, dolphins (is, are) not in search of food; they want friends and fun.
5. Old Greek coins and vases picture a boy and a dolphin who (was, were) friends.
6. People thought the boy (was, were) only part of a story.
7. Dolphins really (is, are) able to enjoy being near people.
8. In 1955 a dolphin named Opo (was, were) the pet of a small New Zealand village.

RULE: **Use *has* when you talk about one.**
Use *have* when you talk about more than one.
Use *had* when you talk about the past.

As far as we know, a dolphin *has* no sense of smell.
Yet dolphins *have* a strange ability to avoid nets.
Three dolphins *had* strange talents.

Write the correct form of the verb *have* on the lines.

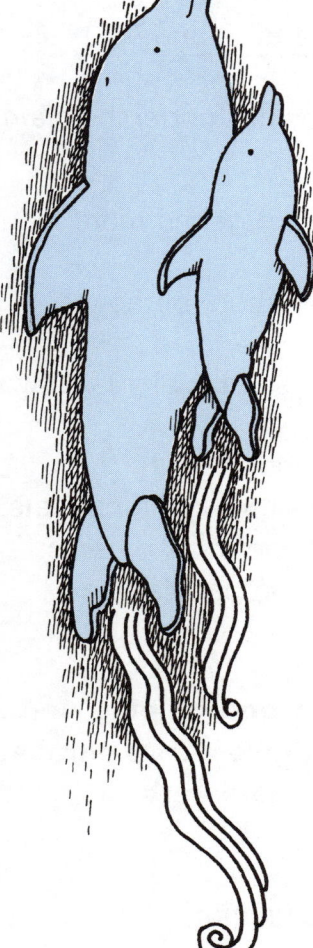

9. Now we know that dolphins ___ a kind of built-in sonar.
10. A dolphin ___ a way of sending out sounds that hit objects and bounce back.
11. With their sonar, dolphins ___ the ability to tell the size and texture of underwater objects.
12. The dolphin also ___ its own language made of whistles, barks, and other sounds.

9. _____   11. _____

10. _____   12. _____

☐ Second Check: Did you write *have* for number 11?

If the underlined verb in each sentence is the correct form, make a check mark (✓) on the line. If the verb is not correct, make an X on the line.

_____ 13. At first baby dolphins *are* always beside their mothers.
_____ 14. As they swim side by side, the tip on one of the baby's flippers *is* always touching the mother's body.
_____ 15. The baby's eye that watches the mother *is* always open.
_____ 16. But the eye on the other side *are* kept closed.
_____ 17. Dolphins *is* very good swimmers.
_____ 18. They *is* able to leap high into the air and dive deep into the water.
_____ 19. I *were* surprised to learn that dolphins invent games.
_____ 20. It *is* a fact that dolphins invented a ring toss game that they play with people.

Write It

Write a short paragraph describing a real animal you know. As often as possible, use the various forms of the verbs *to be* and *to have*. Underline each *to be* or *to have* verb you use.

11   Helping Verbs

Try It

Underline the *helping verb* in this sentence.

Before the summer began, I had looked forward to visiting my uncle.

☐ First Check: Did you underline *had*?

RULE: A verb that is used with the main verb is called a *helping verb*. These verbs are often helping verbs:

be am is are was were been have has had
may can will shall would could should must might

I have gone.   I am going.   I will go.   I can go.
I must go.   I have been going.   I should be going.

Draw one line under the *helping verb* and two lines under the *main verb* in each sentence.

1. My Uncle John probably has enjoyed his pigeons more than any other hobby.
2. By the end of summer I had learned a lot about pigeons.
3. A pigeon does not leave one mate for another.
4. After the female has built a nest of twigs, she usually lays two eggs.
5. In the first weeks the babies are fed pigeon's "milk."
6. Both the male and female can produce this milk in their throats.
7. A baby will put its beak into the beak of one of its parents.
8. Then the parent can pour the "milk" into the baby's beak.

RULE: A main verb can have more than one helping verb. The helping verbs and main verb make a *verb phrase*. The last verb in the phrase is the main verb.

Helping   Main
verbs   verb

We had been going to pigeon races all summer.

Draw one line under the *helping verbs* and two lines under the *main verb* in each sentence.

9. Probably people have been raising pigeons longer than any other bird.

10. At first pigeons may have been raised only for food.
11. In recent times people have been enjoying pigeon races.
12. A homing pigeon might be found far from home.
13. Pigeons have been timed at speeds up to 145 km per hour (90 mph).
14. This swift bird has been carrying messages on flights of over 1,600 km (1,000 miles).
15. During World Wars I and II, homing pigeons may have carried many secret messages.
16. The army must have found these pigeons very useful.
17. The messages can be fastened to the pigeon's back or legs.

☐ Second Check: Did you underline three helping verbs in number 10?

Use It

Do you know when to use the verbs *went* and *gone*? The verb *went* does not need a helping verb.

Uncle John *went* to Blue Lake with the pigeons.

The verb *gone* is always used with a helping verb.

He had *gone* there yesterday to exercise the pigeons.
Had he *gone* before?

Complete each sentence with *went* or *gone*. Write the correct form of the verb on the line.

18. Something had ___ wrong; the pigeons had not returned.
19. "Where have they ___?" I wondered. "Were they caught in the storm?"
20. It was raining hard. I ___ to get my raincoat.
21. While I was ___, Uncle John spotted the pigeons.
22. I ___ to where Uncle John was standing.
23. "They are coming from the west," he said. "They must have ___ around the storm."

18. _____   20. _____   22. _____

19. _____   21. _____   23. _____

Write It

In a short paragraph, describe the problems a homing pigeon might have on a long flight. Use at least five helping verbs.

12 Contractions

Try It

Write the *contraction* of the underlined words in this sentence.

You would probably be surprised at how long it takes to train

a guide dog. _____

☐ First Check: Did you write *You'd* for *You would*?

> **RULE:** A *contraction* is a shortened form of two words. Many contractions are formed with a pronoun and a helping verb. An apostrophe shows where one or more letters have been left out.
>
> I am—I'm   you are—you're   they would—they'd
> they are—they're   we have—we've
> it is—it's   she will—she'll   he had—he'd

Write a contraction on the line to replace the underlined words.

1. The blind girl, Betty, knew she would soon meet her new guide dog.
2. She had come a long way to the Guide Dog Training Center.
3. The dog she will get is a male golden retriever.
4. He has been trained at the Center.
5. Hope is the name they had decided to give Betty's new dog.
6. "You are going to get along fine with Hope," the teacher said to Betty.
7. "I have waited a long time for this," Betty said.
8. Betty worked with Hope until he would answer each of her commands.
9. Betty will be responsible for Hope's care, just as he will be responsible for her safety.

1. _____   4. _____   7. _____

2. _____   5. _____   8. _____

3. _____   6. _____   9. _____

RULE: A *negative contraction* is formed when a helping verb is combined with the word *not*. Here are some negative contractions.

could not—couldn't   is not—isn't   did not—didn't
will not—won't   are not—aren't   cannot—can't

Write a *contraction* to replace the underlined words.

10. A trained guide dog <u>will not</u> cross a busy street until the cars have stopped.
11. Guide dogs <u>do not</u> allow their masters to walk under low-hanging objects.
12. The dog is trained so that it <u>does not</u> get upset in heavy traffic.

10. _____   11. _____   12. _____

☐ Second Check: Did you write *doesn't* for *does not* in number 12?

Fix It

Circle the *contractions* in the following sentences. Write the contractions correctly on the lines.

13. A guide dog must get used to the harness itll wear when guiding a blind owner.
14. A trainer's job doesnt end when the dog is trained.
15. Hes supposed to match the right dog with each blind person.

13. _____   14. _____   15. _____

Use It

The words *they're* and *you're* are contractions that mean *they are* and *you are*. The words *their* and *your* are possessive pronouns. They show ownership.

Circle the correct word in each sentence.

16. Many blind people cannot keep a dog in (they're, their) home.
17. Others find (they're, their) unable to work with a dog.
18. When there is an understanding between a dog and its owner, (they're, their) often the best of friends.

Write It

In a short paragraph, describe what you think a blind person's guide dog must watch for as it walks down a city sidewalk. Use at least three contractions.

Try to use *colorful verbs* when you write. These verbs help to draw word pictures.

> The chimps ate the fruit.   The chimps *gobbled* the fruit.

Colorful verbs can tell you more vividly what is happening.

> The chimp went up the tree.   The chimp *scampered* up the tree.

The verbs *gobbled* and *scampered* tell clearly how the chimp ate and moved.

Circle the more *colorful verb* listed in each sentence. Write the verb on the line.

1. Chimpanzees are known as "noisy apes" because they often (call, screech).
2. They (move, swing) wildly from branch to branch.
3. Chimps (hit, thump) on the trees as they move through the jungle.
4. A baby chimpanzee (clutches, holds) its mother's fur tightly.
5. In time the young chimp (goes, wanders) away from the mother.
6. At any sign of danger, it (scampers, comes) back to her.

1. _____   3. _____   5. _____

2. _____   4. _____   6. _____

Choose a more *colorful verb* from the box for each underlined verb in these sentences. Write your choices on the lines.

scribbles glared squabbled chuckle grasp signal

7. Washoe, the chimp, <u>looked</u> angrily at her teacher.
8. They had just <u>talked</u> about something that Washoe wanted but couldn't have.
9. Washoe was the first chimp to <u>learn</u> a sign language called Ameslan.
10. Washoe knew 175 words and could <u>communicate</u> to others.
11. The chimp sometimes <u>marks</u> quickly with a pen.
12. After playing a joke on the teacher, Washoe will <u>laugh</u> quietly to herself.

7. _____ 9. _____ 11. _____

8. _____ 10. _____ 12. _____

13. Write about an animal you know. Tell how the animal moves. Describe how the animal sleeps and eats. Describe sounds the animal makes. What else does the animal do? Use the most colorful verbs you can think of. Circle each verb you use.

_____

_____

_____

_____

_____

USE THE DICTIONARY

Each entry word in the dictionary is divided into *syllables*. Check the dictionary whenever you're not sure about how to break a word into syllables. Here are some rules that you can follow:

Divide a word so that each syllable has only one vowel sound.

  re/lax/a/tion

Divide a word after a prefix and before a suffix.

  pre/pay   re/do   sing/er   joy/ful

Divide a compound word into its separate words.

  tail/gate   post/card   moon/light

Now divide these words into syllables. Draw a line between the syllables.

14. rework   17. payment   20. suggestion
15. react   18. divide   21. sunshine
16. hillside   19. unhappy   22. sailboat

14 Review

(L 8) Decide whether the underlined verb in each sentence is past, present, or future. Write *past, present*, or *future* on the lines.

1. Bees <u>have lived</u> on earth for many millions of years.
2. In a beehive there <u>are</u> many workers, some drones, and one queen.
3. Bees <u>recognize</u> members of their own hive by smell.
4. Scientists who <u>study</u> bees can tell us much about how a colony works.
5. The scientists <u>watched</u> the bees by using hives built with see-through walls.
6. Future studies <u>will tell</u> us much more about bees.

1. _____   3. _____   5. _____

2. _____   4. _____   6. _____

(L 9) Write the *past tense* of each of these verbs.

7. bring   9. eat   11. find   13. go   15. ring
8. become   10. do   12. know   14. wear

7. _____   10. _____   13. _____

8. _____   11. _____   14. _____

9. _____   12. _____   15. _____

(L 10) Choose the correct form of the verbs *be* and *have* for each sentence. Then write the verb on the line.

16. A successful honeybee colony (has, have) up to 60,000 bees.
17. Some bees (is, are) workers who fly to flowers and bring back food to the colony.
18. They (have, has) nectar in their stomachs as they fly home.
19. Beehives (have, has) workers that take the nectar from other bees. They store it in open cells to dry.
20. When the nectar dries, it (is, are) honey.
21. The bees (has, have) special places to store the honey.

16. _____   18. _____   20. _____

17. _____   19. _____   21. _____

(L 11) Draw one line under the *helping verbs* and two lines under the *main verbs*.

22. In a hive the worker bees are doing several different jobs at any moment.
23. Some will feed the young growing bees.
24. Others will be cleaning out empty cells and preparing them for the queen's eggs.
25. At all times, the opening to the hive is being guarded by other bees.
26. The honeybees can control the temperature in a hive by fanning the air with their wings.

(L 12) Write the *contractions* of the following pairs of words.

27. you are
28. she is
29. will not

30. they would
31. I am
32. had not

33. he has
34. we will
35. can not

27. _____   30. _____   33. _____

28. _____   31. _____   34. _____

29. _____   32. _____   35. _____

(L 13) Choose a *colorful verb* from the box that could replace each of the numbered verbs. Write the colorful verbs on the lines.

raced	plummeted	muttered	gobbled
soared	bounded	gazed	plodded

36. flew _____

37. walked _____

38. jumped _____

39. spoke _____

40. fell _____

41. looked _____

42. ate _____

43. ran _____

15 Test

(L 1) Underline the *singular noun* in each sentence. Circle the *plural noun*.

    1. The children went to the city.
    2. Their parents took them to the zoo.
    3. They saw big cats pacing restlessly in a cage.
    4. Mr. Jefferson pointed to the lions.

(L 4) Write the *subject pronoun* in each sentence.

    5. He said one lion looked tame.
    6. Suddenly it growled loud and long.
    7. "Maybe they aren't so tame," one child said.

    5. _____   6. _____   7. _____

(L 3) Circle the *abbreviation* in each sentence. Write the long form or meaning on the line.

    8. The zoo was on Biscayne Ave., near the park.
    9. Dr. Gianinni was the director of the zoo.
   10. The zoo is open until 9 P.M. every evening.

    8. _____   9. _____   10. _____

(L 5) Write the *possessive noun* or *pronoun* in each sentence.

   11. The children heard Mr. Jefferson's voice again.
   12. "Are your lions tame?" he asked Dr. Gianinni.
   13. "No, they're not tame, and they're not my lions," she said.

   11. _____   12. _____   13. _____

(L 2) Circle the *proper noun* in each sentence.

   14. The director talked about the Edgemont Zoo.
   15. She said she recently returned from Zambia with three great apes.
   16. She said the City Broadcasting System was going to make a film at the zoo.

(L 8) Draw a line under the *verb* in each sentence. Tell whether it is present or past. Write *present* or *past* on the line.

17. Everyone heard screaming near the monkey house.
18. People ran toward the noise.
19. The monkeys escaped from their house!

17. _____   18. _____   19. _____

(L 10) Circle the correct *verb* for each sentence.

20. "The monkeys (is, are) loose," Mr. Jefferson yelled.
21. "This (is, are) an outrage!" Dr. Gianinni complained.
22. "Who (was, were) the foolish person who opened the cage?"
23. "That monkey (has, have) a key," Midge pointed out.
24. "You (has, have) to be kidding," said Mr. Jefferson.
25. "No, she's not," said Dr. Gianinni. "The monkeys (has, have) always wanted their own keys."

(L 11) Underline the *helping verb* in each sentence.

26. "We must stay calm," said Dr. Gianinni.
27. "I might persuade them to return," said Midge.
28. By now the monkeys were running in circles.
29. Maybe Midge could trick the monkeys.
30. She said all the children should climb into the monkey cage.
31. Soon they were jumping around inside the cage.

(L 12) Underline the *contraction* in each sentence. Then write the two words it stands for.

32. The monkeys didn't understand what was happening.
33. They hadn't ever seen such an unusual thing.
34. "They're so curious, they will come over to see more," said Midge.
35. "I'll be a monkey's uncle," said Mr. Jefferson.
36. It wasn't long before the monkeys were crowding into the cage.
37. "I've never seen so much monkey business," said Mr. Jefferson.

32. _____   34. _____   36. _____

33. _____   35. _____   37. _____

Try It

Circle the *adjectives* in the following sentences.

Maria lives on a beautiful farm.
Stanley lives in a big city.
They write each other many letters.

☐   First Check: Did you circle *beautiful, big*, and *many*?

RULE: *Adjectives* **are descriptive words. They are words that** *describe, picture*, **or** *tell more* **about people, places, or things.**

young boys	*blue* skies	*some* clouds	*wet* grass
older girls	*wide* street	*pretty* words	*eight* cars

Read the letter. Circle the *adjective* in each of the following sentences. Then write it on the line.

Dear Maria,

1. New York is really a great city.
2. On Thursday I went for a long walk.
3. New buildings are going up all the time.
4. First the old ones have to be torn down.
5. This, of course, leaves an enormous hole in the ground.
6. The workers have to build for many months before they reach street level again.
7. They usually build the frame with huge beams of steel.
8. First they finish the whole frame.
9. Then they work from the first floor up.
10. The buildings take many years to complete.
11. Sometimes the outside is mirrored glass.
12. On clear days the glass glistens in the sun.

Your friend,
Stanley

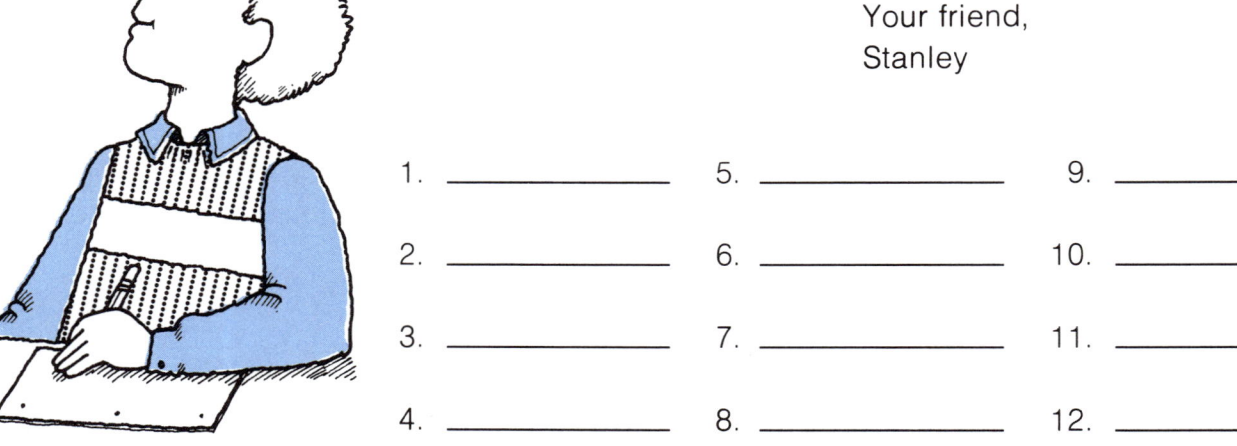

1. _____   5. _____   9. _____

2. _____   6. _____   10. _____

3. _____   7. _____   11. _____

4. _____   8. _____   12. _____

34

Think of *adjectives* that make sense in these sentences. Write the *adjectives* on the lines.

13. Stanley has always lived in a ___ city.
14. Maria lives in Vermont near ___ fields and streams.
15. They met only once on a ___ vacation in Boston.
16. Through their letters they have become ___ friends.

13. _____   15. _____

14. _____   16. _____

> **RULE: More than one *adjective* can be used with a single noun.**
>
> a cold, clear day   a red and white shirt

Circle the *adjectives* and underline the *nouns* they go with.

Dear Stan,

17. Thank you for the long and interesting letter.
18. As you know, there are no tall glass buildings here.
19. Yesterday I went into the forest and found a round wooden house.
20. The house was built across a narrow green brook.
21. It was built by smart little beavers.

Add a second *adjective* to each of the following sentences. Write the adjectives on the lines.

22. Beavers have ___ sharp teeth.
23. To build their homes, they cut down ___ little trees.
24. Even the ___ baby beavers help with the work.
25. The doors to their homes are all under water, so they have to be ___ quick swimmers.
26. Their ___ broad tails help them get around in the water.
27. Maybe you'll leave that ___ old city and visit me.

22. _____   24. _____   26. _____

23. _____   25. _____   27. _____

Write It   Write a short paragraph describing a house that you would like to live in. Use two adjectives in each sentence.

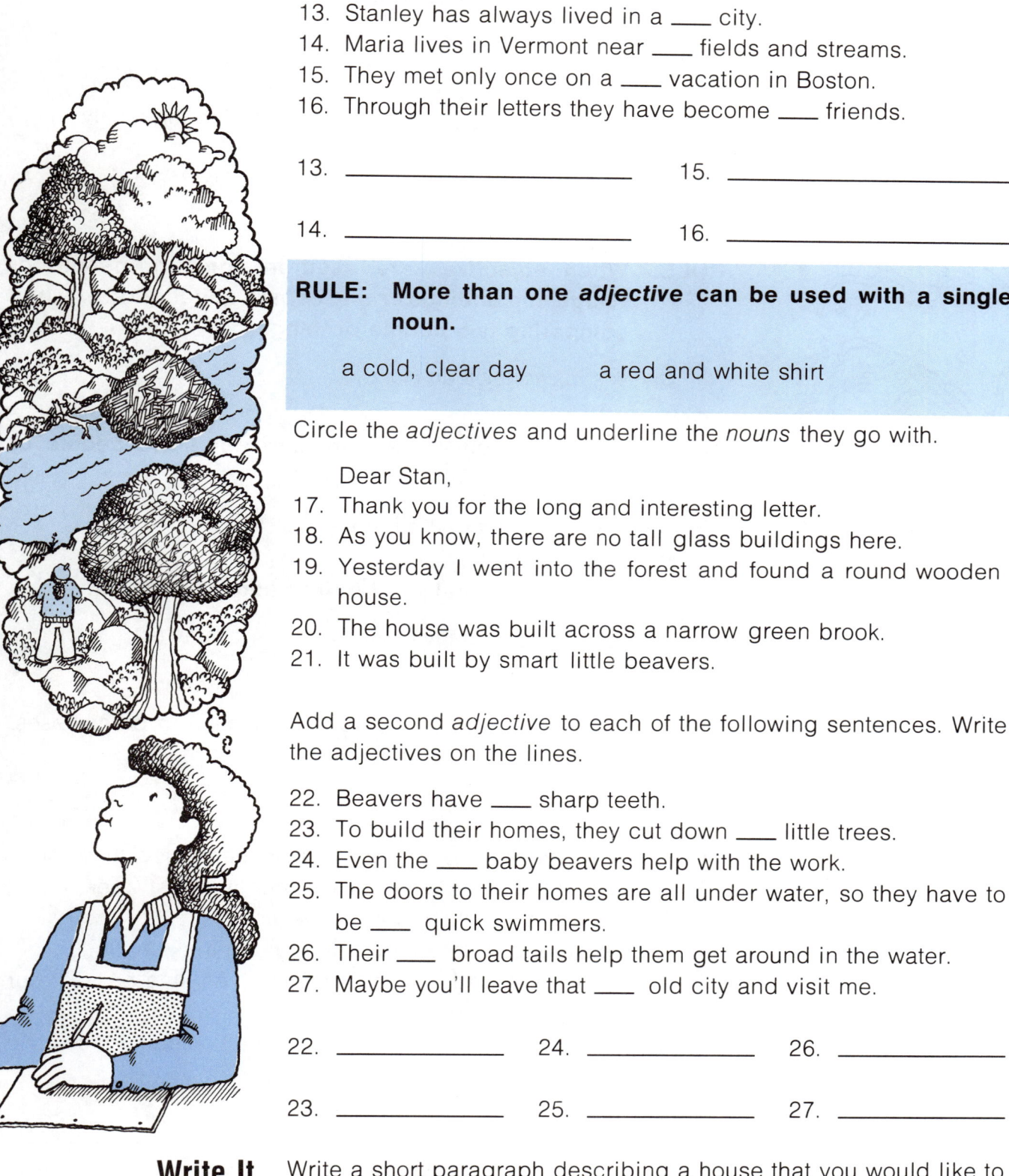

Try It

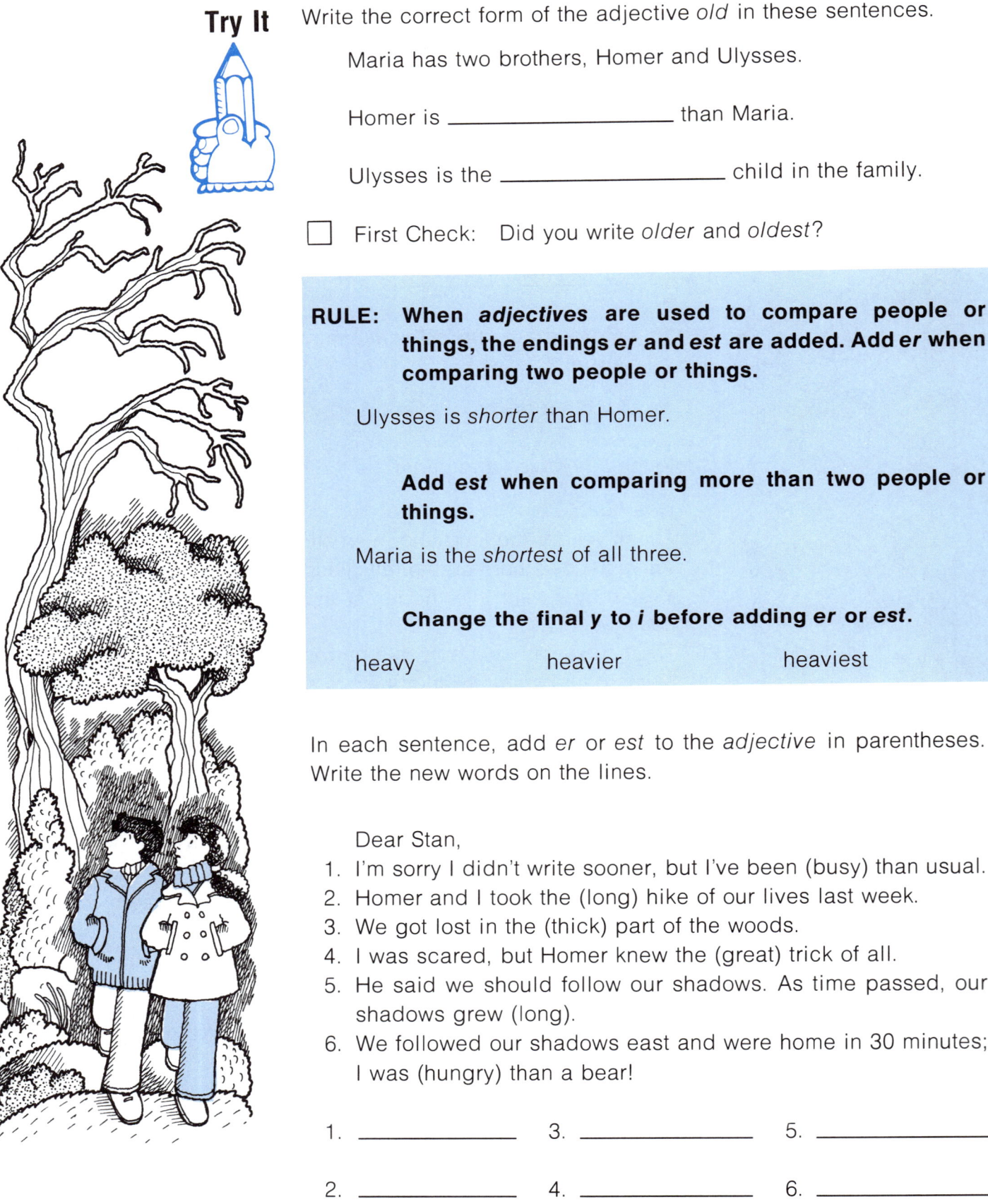

Write the correct form of the adjective *old* in these sentences.

Maria has two brothers, Homer and Ulysses.

Homer is _____ than Maria.

Ulysses is the _____ child in the family.

☐ First Check: Did you write *older* and *oldest*?

RULE: When *adjectives* are used to compare people or things, the endings *er* and *est* are added. Add *er* when comparing two people or things.

Ulysses is *shorter* than Homer.

Add *est* when comparing more than two people or things.

Maria is the *shortest* of all three.

Change the final *y* to *i* before adding *er* or *est*.

heavy   heavier   heaviest

In each sentence, add *er* or *est* to the *adjective* in parentheses. Write the new words on the lines.

Dear Stan,
1. I'm sorry I didn't write sooner, but I've been (busy) than usual.
2. Homer and I took the (long) hike of our lives last week.
3. We got lost in the (thick) part of the woods.
4. I was scared, but Homer knew the (great) trick of all.
5. He said we should follow our shadows. As time passed, our shadows grew (long).
6. We followed our shadows east and were home in 30 minutes; I was (hungry) than a bear!

1. _____   3. _____   5. _____

2. _____   4. _____   6. _____

36

Adjectives

Use It

The verbs *have* and *has* are often confused. Use *has* with *he*, *she*, *it*, and singular nouns.

He *has* two ropes.   One rope *has* two knots.

Use have with *I, you, we, they*, and plural nouns.

I *have* old sneakers.   My sneakers *have* big holes.

Complete each sentence with *have* or *has*.

Dear Maria,

7. I _____ never used the shadow trick for finding myself in New York.

8. The subways _____ given me the most trouble.

9. The sun _____ never shone down there.

10. _____ you ever ridden on a subway?

For each of the following sentences, write the correct *comparing form* of the adjective.

11. Sometimes the subways are the (easy) way to get around.
12. They are much (fast) than buses.
13. There are times when the (hard) thing is knowing which way you're going.
14. Last week I hopped on the (noisy) subway in the city.
15. It was the (quick) ride ever.
16. Unfortunately, I had taken the (fast) train in the wrong direction.
17. Sometimes walking slowly is the (smart) way to go.

11. _____   14. _____   16. _____

12. _____   15. _____   17. _____

13. _____

Write It

Write a short paragraph describing a time when you got lost. How did you feel? How did you find your way back? Use adjectives ending in *er* and *est* to describe what it was like.

18 Using More and Most

Try It

Complete each sentence with the correct form of the adjective.

This autumn has been _____ than last autumn. (cold)

It couldn't have been a _____ season. (beautiful)

☐ First Check: Did you write *colder* and *more beautiful*?

> **RULE:** **The words *more* and *most* are used with adjectives to compare people and things. Use *more* to compare two people or things. Use *most* to compare more than two people or things. *More* and *most* are usually used with adjectives that have *three* or more syllables.**
>
> | smart | smarter | smartest |
> |---|---|---|
> | valuable | more valuable | most valuable |

Write the correct form of the *adjective*. Use *er* and *est* or *more* and *most*.

Dear Stan,

1. Today is Thanksgiving, and I couldn't be (excited).
2. Ulysses, the (old) of my two brothers, is back from college.
3. He has the (difficult) job of the year—killing the turkey.
4. Is that the (terrible) thing you have ever heard?
5. Perhaps it is (easy) for me because I grew up on a farm.
6. It is probably the (painful) part of farm life.
7. I think our own beans, squash, apples, and grapes are (delicious) than turkey.
8. They are certainly the (colorful) things on the table.
9. I hope you have the (wonderful) Thanksgiving ever.

> Your friend,
> Maria

1. _____   6. _____

2. _____   7. _____

3. _____   8. _____

4. _____   9. _____

5. _____

Fix It

Each of these sentences contains an *adjective* in an incorrect form. Rewrite the adjective correctly on the line.

Dear Maria,

10. Your letter has made me think more hard about Thanksgiving.
11. Thanksgiving in New York was more nicer than usual.
12. We went to the fancier restaurant in the whole city.
13. But we didn't have the most greatest dinner.

10. _____   12. _____

11. _____   13. _____

Complete each sentence with the correct form of the adjective. Write the correct adjectives on the lines.

14. Let me tell you about Thanksgiving dinner; it was the (mixed-up) meal of the century.
15. Dad forgot to take the turkey out of the freezer. When we tried to cook it, it was (hard) than a rock.
16. We decided to eat out. But each restaurant was (crowded) than the last.
17. We waited two hours in one place that was (hot) than a greenhouse.
18. Then we heard the (horrible) news of all: They had run out of turkey.
19. Mom was furious. Dad was (angry) than Mom.
20. The (simple) thing to do was to go home and eat peanut butter.
21. At home we saw that the turkey was ready to cook. We had the (late) Thanksgiving dinner on record.
22. It was great! Much (delicious) than peanut butter.

14. _____   17. _____   20. _____

15. _____   18. _____   21. _____

16. _____   19. _____   22. _____

Write It

Write a short paragraph about the most unusual meal you can remember. Write at least three sentences with adjectives that compare people or things.

Try It

Circle the *adverb* in this sentence.

The cars and trucks crept slowly down the street.

☐ First Check: Did you circle *slowly*?

RULE: *Adverbs* **are descriptive words.** *Adverbs* **work with verbs by telling** *how, when*, **or** *where* **an action occurs.** *Adverbs* **often end in** *ly*.

How	When	Where
selfishly	today	downtown
luckily	sometimes	there
surprisingly	early	somewhere

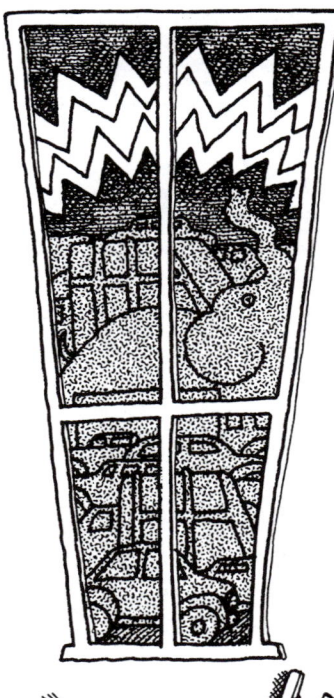

Circle the *adverb* in each of these sentences.

Dear Maria,

1. New York is always crowded with cars.
2. They all honk loudly.
3. And that certainly doesn't help.
4. I sometimes wish they would all leave.
5. Manhattan, as you probably know, is an island.
6. Yesterday I learned that Manhattan has 17 bridges.
7. With any luck, people will start using them more often.
8. I really don't care where the cars go.
9. I simply want to get a good night's sleep.
10. That's hard when a million cars are honking angrily.
11. I dreamed about a wounded elephant recently.
12. Frightened, I woke up; a garbage truck was roaring wildly on the street.

Your friend,
Stanley

RULE: An *adverb* **can often be formed by adding** *ly* **to an adjective.**

correct   correctly

The final *y* **of an adjective changes to** *i* **before adding** *ly*.

lucky   luckily

Change the adjective in each sentence to an *adverb*. Write the *adverb* on the line.

Dear Stan,

13. We (sure) don't have noise problems like you.
14. And I can (hard) believe there are so many bridges.
15. Around here we (definite) don't need that many.
16. The two that we do have make people drive (slow).
17. They were both (sturdy) built.
18. But they are covered bridges that have been kept (careful) since the 1800s.

13. _____   15. _____   17. _____

14. _____   16. _____   18. _____

Circle the *adverb* in each of these sentences. Then write whether it tells *where, when,* or *how.*

19. Covered bridges were once the most popular bridges.
20. They were built here before cars were invented.
21. Foolishly I thought they were covered because it looks nice.
22. The covers were really built to protect both the bridge and the traveler.
23. They were places to wait quietly during a storm.
24. Sometimes I think covered bridges are like tunnels in the sky.

Your friend,
Maria

19. _____   21. _____   23. _____

20. _____   22. _____   24. _____

Write It   Write a short paragraph about a bridge you have crossed. Write at least three sentences with adverbs that describe *how, when,* or *where.*

20 Adverbial Phrases

Try It

In each sentence circle *the group of words* that acts as an *adverb*.

The first robin was seen this morning.
It flew into the kitchen.

☐ First Check: Did you circle *this morning* and *into the kitchen*?

RULE: *Adverbs* are words that tell about verbs. *Adverbs* tell *how, when*, or *where* an action occurs.

When	**Where**	**How**
It flew *today*.	It flew *upstairs*.	It flew *quickly*.

A group of words can act as an adverb.

How	**When**	**Where**
with ease	during lunch	in the garden

Each of the following sentences contains an adverb or a group of words that acts as an adverb. Circle *the adverbs*.

Dear Stanley,
1. Spring has finally arrived.
2. The last snow melted in April.
3. The birds are returning from the south.
4. Sometimes they can find their old nests.
5. If people have disturbed the nests even slightly, the birds will build new ones.
6. They easily gather twigs and leaves.
7. They use pieces of string and paper that have been left on the ground.
8. They work all day.
9. One robin stole Mom's handkerchief off the line.

Use It

The words *good* and *well* are often confused. *Good* is an *adjective*. It is used to describe a *person, place*, or *thing*.

He is a *good* student.   *Good* work takes time.

Well is an adverb that tells how.

He works *well*.   He also writes *well*.

42

Circle the correct word to complete each sentence.

10. The birds I have seen are very (good, well) builders.
11. Their nests are always built (good, well).
12. They do (good, well) to choose safe spots for the nests.
13. A comfortable nest means they will sing (good, well).
14. It would be (good, well) if you could come up here and see all my birds.
15. Thank you for your last letter; you write so (good, well).

> Love,
> Maria

Read these sentences. From the box, choose the *adverb* or *group of words* that makes sense in each sentence. Write the words on the lines.

in the city	completely	in 10 years
for some reason	unfortunately	certainly

Dear Maria,

16. Here ___ we have building problems too.
17. ___ people want to tear down the nicest old buildings.
18. ___ they think "new" is "better."
19. It would ___ be nicer if they just fixed the buildings again.
20. I would like to see all the old buildings ___ cleaned up.
21. Otherwise ___ they will all be gone.

> Love,
> Stanley

16. _____   18. _____   20. _____

17. _____   19. _____   21. _____

☐ Second Check: Did you use a different adverb or group of words in each sentence?

Write It   Write a short paragraph about visiting a friend of yours. Write at least three sentences with groups of words acting as adverbs.

21 Writing Pad

Complete each of the following sentences with *two adjectives.*

1. Maria's house was _____ and _____.

2. Stanley liked the _____ _____ trees.

3. _____ _____ birds flew from tree to tree.

4. A _____ stream ran behind the _____ house.

5. The sky was _____ and _____.

6. The _____ forest was as _____ as Stan had

   imagined.

Add an *adverb* to complete each sentence. Your adverb should answer the word in parentheses.

7. Stanley and Maria walked _____.
   (where)

8. A rabbit ran _____ across the field.
   (how)

9. Stanley wanted to chase it _____.
   (where)

10. _____ they climbed over some rocks.
    (when)

11. Maria did it much more _____ than Stan.
    (how)

12. They could see a river _____.
    (where)

13. They would be there _____.
    (when)

14. Write a short paragraph about the river. Use some of the following words to start phrases that act as adverbs.

in	on	for	with
at	under	before	between

44

_____

_____

_____

_____

_____

USE THE DICTIONARY

The *guide words* at the top of each dictionary page will help you find words quickly. The guide words tell you the first and last entry words on a dictionary page. The first entry at the top of the left-hand column is *kingfisher*. The last entry at the bottom of the right-hand column is *knew*.

The *guide words* look like this.

kingfisher	knew
king•fish•er (king′ fish ər) *n.* A brightly-colored bird with a short tail and strong bill that usually eats fish.	**kitch•en** (kich ən) *n.* A room where food is prepared and cooked.
kit (kit) *n.* A collection of tools or equipment for some special purpose.	**knew** (n[y]oo) *v.* Past form of the verb *know*.

Circle the words that would be on this dictionary page.

kink	knack	knuckle
kind	knee	kissing
kimono	kite	kilt
knot	knight	Kenya

22 Review

(L 16) Circle the *adjective* in each sentence. Then draw an arrow to the noun the adjective describes. Write the adjective on the line.

1. New York is not a new city.

2. Nor is it as old as the hills.

3. Busy people are rushing everywhere.

4. There is always a heavy flow of traffic.

5. Great buses nose their way among the cars.

6. Shiny buildings gleam in the morning.

7. Tired workers hurry home at night.

8. The stores are filled with beautiful things.

9. Shoppers buy expensive gifts.

1. _____   6. _____

2. _____   7. _____

3. _____   8. _____

4. _____   9. _____

5. _____

(L 17, 18) Write the correct form of each *adjective* on the line.

10. Days in the city seem (short) than in the country.
11. The nights in the country are (quiet) than in the city.
12. In the country the stars seem clearer and (beautiful).
13. Of all the nice things about the country, the clean air is the (wonderful).
14. On the (hot) day of the year I would like to be in the country.
15. Of course city life is often (expensive) than country life.

10. _____   13. _____

11. _____   14. _____

12. _____   15. _____

(L 19)   Write the *adverb* from each sentence on the line.

16. City movies are usually newer.
17. Unfortunately there are long lines.
18. City life changes quickly.
19. People attend museums and concerts frequently.
20. Theaters are certainly a nice part of city life.
21. Often jobs are more available in a city.

16. _____   18. _____   20. _____

17. _____   19. _____   21. _____

(L 20)   Underline the group of words in each sentence that tells *where, when,* or *how*. Write whether the word group tells where, when, or how.

22. Next winter Maria plans to visit Stanley.
23. She plans to travel by bus.
24. She will have many surprises during her trip.
25. At the theater Stanley and Maria will see four funny movies.
26. They will eat food from six countries.
27. She will ice skate on a rink.
28. For four days she will have a wonderful time.

22. _____   25. _____   28. _____

23. _____   26. _____

24. _____   27. _____

23 Types of Sentences

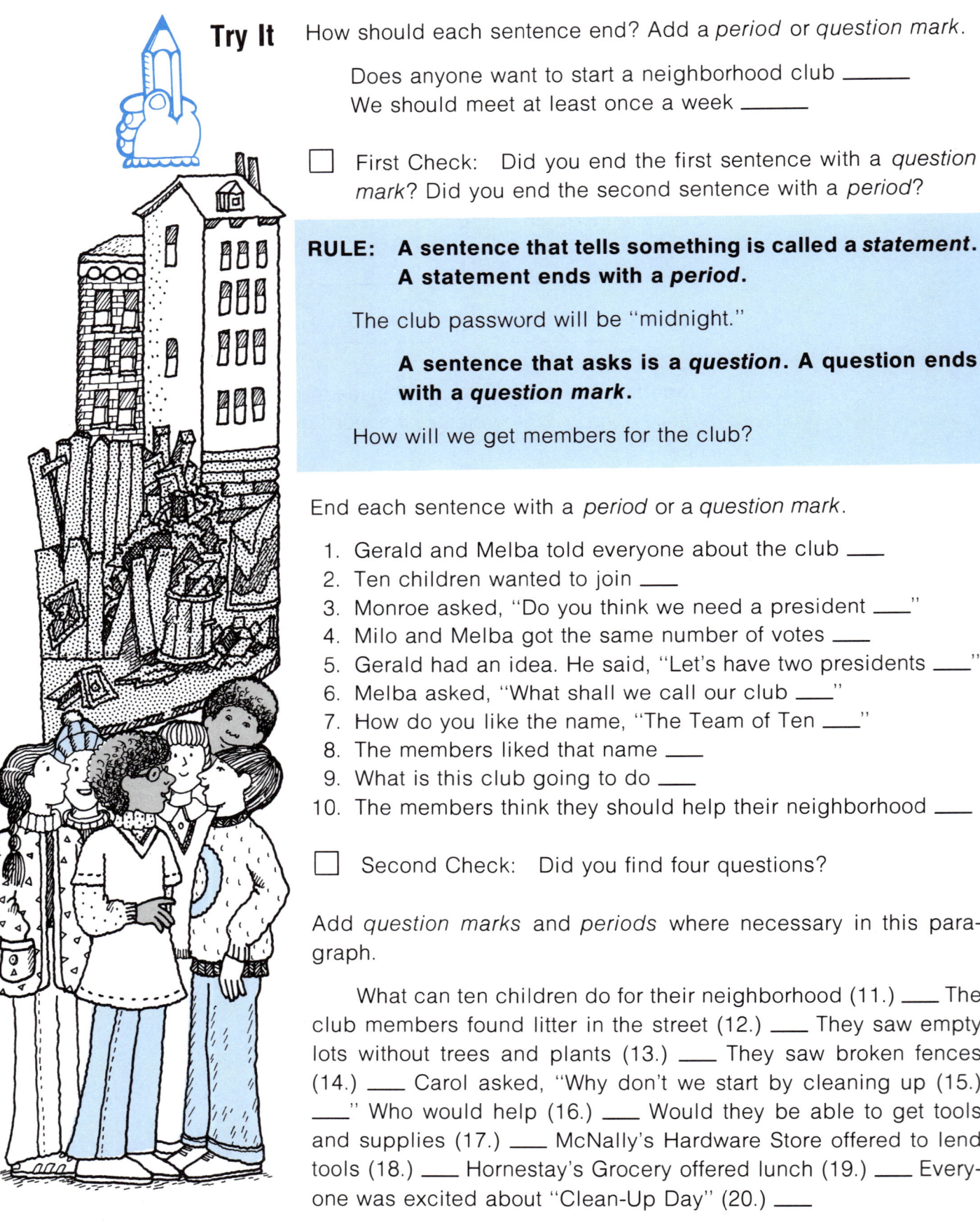

Try It How should each sentence end? Add a *period* or *question mark*.

Does anyone want to start a neighborhood club _____
We should meet at least once a week _____

☐ First Check: Did you end the first sentence with a *question mark*? Did you end the second sentence with a *period*?

RULE: A sentence that tells something is called a *statement*. A statement ends with a *period*.

The club password will be "midnight."

A sentence that asks is a *question*. A question ends with a *question mark*.

How will we get members for the club?

End each sentence with a *period* or a *question mark*.

1. Gerald and Melba told everyone about the club ____
2. Ten children wanted to join ____
3. Monroe asked, "Do you think we need a president ____"
4. Milo and Melba got the same number of votes ____
5. Gerald had an idea. He said, "Let's have two presidents ____"
6. Melba asked, "What shall we call our club ____"
7. How do you like the name, "The Team of Ten ____"
8. The members liked that name ____
9. What is this club going to do ____
10. The members think they should help their neighborhood ____

☐ Second Check: Did you find four questions?

Add *question marks* and *periods* where necessary in this paragraph.

What can ten children do for their neighborhood (11.) ____ The club members found litter in the street (12.) ____ They saw empty lots without trees and plants (13.) ____ They saw broken fences (14.) ____ Carol asked, "Why don't we start by cleaning up (15.) ____" Who would help (16.) ____ Would they be able to get tools and supplies (17.) ____ McNally's Hardware Store offered to lend tools (18.) ____ Hornestay's Grocery offered lunch (19.) ____ Everyone was excited about "Clean-Up Day" (20.) ____

48

RULE: A sentence that shows very strong feeling ends with an *exclamation point* (!). This type of sentence is called an *exclamation*.

On Clean-up Day, Gerald said, "I've never worked so hard! Our block looks beautiful!"

End each sentence with a *period, question mark*, or *exclamation point*.

21. By five o'clock The Team of Ten was very tired ___
22. Where had the day gone ___
23. A short lunch was their only break ___
24. Gerald asked, "Have you ever seen this street so clean ___"
25. There wasn't one can or scrap of paper anywhere ___
26. Morning glories had been painted on the garbage cans ___
27. Wow! I've never been this tired in my life ___
28. I can't believe we did this all by ourselves ___
29. Do you think we can keep it clean around here ___
30. If everyone helps, you bet we can ___

Write It Write two statements that give your ideas about a club meeting place and a club project.

_____

_____

Write two questions about joining a club.

_____

_____

Write an exclamation that tells what you might say when:

Melba drops a flowerpot next to you.
Mrs. McNally is about to sit on wet paint.

_____

_____

Try It

Draw one line under the *subject* of this sentence. Draw two lines under the *predicate*.

The neighbors admired the club's work.

☐ First Check: Did you draw one line under *neighbors*? Did you draw two lines under *admired*?

> **RULE:** The *simple subject* of a sentence is a noun or pronoun that tells who or what does something. The simple subject is who or what the sentence is about.
> The *simple predicate* is the verb that tells **what** the subject is or does.
>
> | | Subject | Predicate | |
> |---|---|---|---|
> | (The old) | neighborhood | looked | (like new.) |
> | (The) | trash | was gone. | |
> | | Everyone | smiled. | |

Underline the *simple subject* and circle the *simple predicate* of each sentence.

The <u>club</u> (wanted) more projects.

IDEA DAY!

1. Monroe had a great idea.
2. He suggested "Idea Day."
3. Neighborhood people wrote their ideas on paper.
4. The members of the club collected the papers.
5. Many people asked for a talent show.
6. Other people suggested a flea market.
7. The club members wanted a food festival.
8. "We should have a street fair."
9. "A street fair uses all the ideas."

☐ Second Check: Did you underline *members* in sentence 4? Did you circle *collected* in sentence 4?

> **RULE:** The *complete subject* of a sentence is all the words that make up the subject part of the sentence. The complete subject tells more about the simple subject. The *complete predicate* of a sentence tells more about the simple predicate.

50

	COMPLETE SUBJECT	COMPLETE PREDICATE

EVERYONE IN THE NEIGHBORHOOD TALKED ABOUT THE FAIR.

SIMPLE SUBJECT

SIMPLE PREDICATE

Underline the *complete subject* in each of these sentences. Circle the *complete predicate*.

10. The Team of Ten planned for the fair.
11. They received permission to close off a street.
12. The young people set a date—July 27.
13. Many people in the neighborhood gave things for the garage sale.
14. The children cooked their most special dishes.
15. The excited club members set up colorful stands.

Use It

How do you know whether to use *is* or *are* with the word *there*? Many sentences begin with the word *there*. The subject of these sentences comes after *there is* or *there are*. To find the subject of these sentences, drop the word *there* and rearrange the sentence. Put the verb after the simple subject.

SUBJECT

There are *many people* at the fair. Many people are at the fair.

SUBJECT

There is a *juggler* on the corner. A juggler is on the corner.

Use *there is* or *there was* when the subject is singular. Use *there are* or *there were* when the subject is plural.

Find the *subject* in each sentence. Is it singular or plural? Cross out the incorrect word.

16. There (is, are) people at the fair from many neighborhoods.
17. There (is, are) a man with his face painted green.
18. There (was, were) a Spanish band on the corner.
19. There (was, were) a silver lion for sale.
20. "There (is, are) something for everyone," one man shouted.
21. There (was, were) never such a wonderful street fair.

Write It

Write three sentences that tell about a fair you have been to or would like to see. Draw one line under the simple subject in each sentence. Draw two lines under the simple predicate.

Try It

Write the two *subjects* of this sentence.

Monroe and Rebecca were excited about the street fair.

_____

☐   First Check: Did you write *Monroe* and *Rebecca*?

> **RULE:**   **Some sentences have a *compound subject*. A compound subject is two subjects joined by the word *and* or *or*.**
>
> The *streets* and the *sidewalks* were crowded with people.

Underline the *subjects* of each sentence.

1. The children and neighbors set up stands for the fair.
2. Food and drink were sold on one side of the street.
3. The flea market and the talent show were held on the other side.
4. Egg rolls, pizza, and tacos could be bought at the fair.
5. Mr. McNally and Mrs. Hornestay sold tickets for a prize drawing.
6. A bicycle and basket would be the prize.

> **RULE:**   **Some sentences have a *compound predicate*. A compound predicate is two verbs. It tells two different things that the subject of a sentence does.**
>
> Melba *sold* food and *gave* change.

Write the *predicates* of these sentences on the lines.

7. Marcel and Gerald tasted the egg rolls and drank soda.
8. Bianca walked around and picked up garbage.
9. People at the flea market bought and traded old things.
10. Everyone danced and clapped with the band.
11. Then Mrs. Koslofsky rang a bell and called for attention.
12. The crowd stood still and waited.

7. _____ _____   10. _____ _____

8. _____ _____   11. _____ _____

9. _____ _____   12. _____ _____

52

Predicates

☐ Second Check: Did you write *bought* and *traded* as the predicates of sentence 9?

Combine each pair of sentences. Write one sentence with a *compound subject* or a *compound predicate*.

Everyone held his or her breath.
Everyone waited.

Everyone held his or her breath and waited.

13. Mrs. Hornestay drew the name from a jar.
    Mr. McNally drew the name from a jar.

14. Mrs. Hornestay opened the paper.
    Mrs. Hornestay read it.

15. The winner of the bike is Ms. Allen.
    The new owner of the bike is Ms. Allen.

16. Ms. Allen got on the bike.
    Ms. Allen rode it.

17. "There are people who deserve this bike more than I," Ms. Allen said.
    "There are people who need this bike more than I," she said.

18. "The neighborhood gives this bike to the Team of Ten."
    "I give this bike to the Team of Ten."

Write It   Write a paragraph that tells more about this street fair. Use one sentence with more than one subject. Use one sentence with more than one predicate.

Try It

Rewrite the sentences correctly. Make the predicate *agree* with the subject.

The club members wants something to do.

_____

Monroe have an idea.

_____

☐ First Check: Did you change *wants* to *want*? Did you change *have* to *has*?

RULE: **The subject and predicate of a sentence must *agree*. A singular subject (one person, place, or thing) takes the singular form of the verb in the predicate. A plural subject takes the plural form of the verb.**

Singular	**Plural**
Monroe tells his plan.	The children tell their plan.
One old man needs help.	Many older people need help.

Underline the subject of each sentence. Then write the correct verb on the line.

1. Melba (prints, print) posters.
2. Soon the calls will (comes, come) in.
3. Many older people (wants, want) help.
4. Marcel and Monroe (goes, go) to the store for Mrs. Ragina Quinn.
5. She (tips, tip) them a quarter for their help.
6. The boys (gives, give) the money to the club.
7. Milo (walks, walk) Mr. King's dog.
8. Kristi (plays, play) cards with Mr. Winter and Mrs. Kougentakis.
9. Then Mr. Adams (calls, call); he wants some help.
10. Everyone (looks, look) at each other.
11. Mr. Adams (hasn't, haven't) been out of his house for years.
12. No one (has, have) ever seen the inside of his house.

1. _____   3. _____   5. _____

2. _____   4. _____   6. _____

54

Agreement

7. _____   9. _____   11. _____

8. _____   10. _____   12. _____

☐ Second Check: In sentence 8 did you underline *Kristi*? Did you write the verb *plays*?

RULE: Use the *plural form* of the verb in sentences with compound subjects.

Milo, Kristi, and Gerald are afraid.
They refuse to go to his house.

Write the correct form of the verb.

13. Melba and Milo (is, are) the presidents of the club.
14. She and he (decides, decide) who will go.
15. Bianca and Monroe (offers, offer) to take the job.

13. _____   14. _____   15. _____

Fix It

Circle the *incorrect verb* in each sentence. Write the verb correctly on the line.

16. Everyone thinks Mr. Adams is strange because he never come out.
17. Monroe like mysteries; he wants to get to know Mr. Adams.
18. Carmen thinks he have a hidden treasure or something.
19. They rings Mr. Adam's bell; a small, secret door opens.
20. A note and some money slides out; the children read the note.
21. "Please get me three kittens," it say.

16. _____   18. _____   20. _____

17. _____   19. _____   21. _____

Write It

Why do you think Mr. Adams wants kittens? Write three sentences that tell why he wants them. Underline each subject you write. Draw a circle around each predicate. Remember that your subject and verb must agree.

Try It

Write these sentences as one sentence.

The small door slammed.   The secret door slammed.

_____

☐ First Check: Did you write: *The small, secret door slammed?*

RULE: There are many ways to combine sentences. You can combine sentences by using more than one adjective.

The brave children walked home. ⎫
⎬ The brave, helpful children walked home.
The helpful children walked home. ⎭

You can combine sentences by using more than one adverb.

The children walked slowly. ⎫
⎬ The children walked slowly and quietly.
The children walked quietly. ⎭

Combine each pair of sentences. Write the new sentences.

1. Bianca told the club about the unusual door. Bianca told the club about the secret door.

_____

2. Toby had three kittens. Toby had black kittens.

_____

3. The children talked nervously. They talked excitedly.

_____

RULE: You can combine similar sentences that have groups of words that tell *where*, *when*, or *how*.

The children went to Toby's house. ⎫
⎬ The children went to Toby's house at two o'clock.
The children went at two o'clock. ⎭

Circle the group of words in each sentence that tells *where, when,* or *how.* Then combine the pair of sentences.

4. The kittens were playing happily.
   The kittens were in Toby's basement.

   _____

5. Toby finally said she would lend them the kittens.
   She would lend them the kittens for a few days.

   _____

6. A few minutes later Toby and Bianca left.
   Toby and Bianca left for Mr. Adams' house.

   _____

Use It

The word *doesn't* means *does not.* The word *don't* means *do not.*
Use *doesn't* when you talk about one person, place, or thing.
   Monroe *doesn't* want the kitten to be hurt.
Use *don't* when you talk about more than one person, place, or thing. Use *don't* with the words *you* and *I.*
   I *don't* think Mr. Adams will hurt them.
   You *don't* have to worry.
   The kittens *don't* mind him at all.
Complete each sentence with *doesn't* or *don't.*

7. Toby ____ want to ring the bell.
8. "You ____ have to be afraid," Bianca says. "Ring the bell."
9. Mr. Adams ____ answer the door right away.
10. He thinks the children are selling something. "I ____ want any," he says.
11. "We brought three kittens," Bianca said, "but we ____ want you to hurt them."
12. "I would never hurt a kitten," Mr. Adams said. "____ you want to come in and see what I'm planning to do?"

7. _____   9. _____   11. _____

8. _____   10. _____   12. _____

Write It

Can you remember the last time you were afraid? What did you do about your fear? Write a paragraph that tells.

Every complete sentence has a subject and a predicate. Sometimes a group of words that begins with a capital letter and ends with a period is not a sentence. These groups of words are called *fragments*.

Sentence	**Fragment**
Bianca and Monroe walked into the house.	Walked into the house. **(NO SUBJECT)**
The surprised children looked around.	The surprised children. **(NO PREDICATE)**

Tell whether each of the following groups of words is a sentence or fragment. Write *sentence* or *fragment* on the line.

1. Mr. Adams' living room was a circus.
2. Posters hung on the walls.
3. Played circus music.
4. Monkeys did tricks on the ceiling.
5. Dogs, cats, birds, and mice.
6. Flashed over the center ring.

1. _____ 3. _____ 5. _____

2. _____ 4. _____ 6. _____

Now rewrite three of the fragments so they are complete sentences. Add a subject or a predicate to each fragment to make it complete.

7. _____

_____

8. _____

_____

9. _____

_____

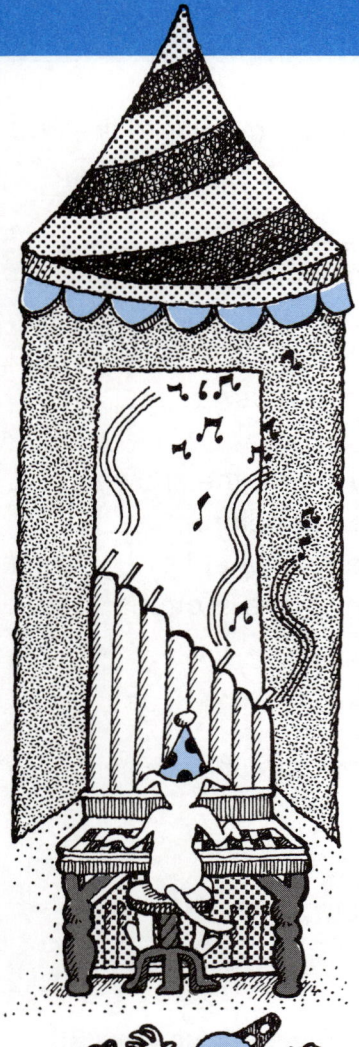

Sometimes a sentence is very long and tries to say too much. It is called a *run-on sentence*. A confusing run-on sentence can be made into shorter sentences.

> Mr. Adams jumped into the center ring and he called for attention by loudly clapping his hands and then all the animals stopped doing tricks and they watched him carefully.

> Mr. Adams jumped into the center ring. He called for attention by loudly clapping his hands. All the animals stopped doing tricks. They watched him carefully.

Write each of these run-on sentences as three sentences.

10. Mr. Adams told Bianca and Toby to sit down and he said there was going to be a show and they could hardly believe what they were seeing.

_____

_____

_____

11. The organ played the monkeys jumped on the dogs' backs and they all paraded around the room.

_____

_____

_____

USE THE DICTIONARY

Many prefixes are listed as entry words in the dictionary.

> **dis-,** a prefix meaning: 1 opposite of, as in *distrust*. 2 reverse of, as in *disengage*.
> **in-,** a prefix meaning: 1 not; the opposite of, as in *incomplete*. 2 in; into; within, toward; as in *inhabit* and *indoors*.
> **un-,** a prefix meaning: not; the opposite of; as in *unfair* and *unkind*.

(L 23) Add a *period,* a *question mark*, or an *exclamation point* to the end of each sentence.

1. The show was the most exciting ever _____
2. Have you ever seen such wonderful tricks _____
3. The monkeys flew all over the place _____
4. Bianca and Toby ate popcorn _____
5. I can't believe this; it's our own special circus _____
6. Why do you need the kittens _____
7. Mr. Adams told them he wanted a new act for the show _____
8. Why haven't you ever invited anyone here before _____
9. He said, "I didn't think anyone cared about what I did _____"
10. We would have come a long time ago to see a circus _____
11. Where did you get this circus _____

(L 24) Write the *simple subject* and the *simple predicate* of each sentence on the lines.

12. I owned a small circus once.
13. We traveled all over the country with our show.
14. Then the circus went out of business.
15. Only a big circus could survive.
16. The club members felt bad for Mr. Adams.

Subject	Predicate
12. _____	_____
13. _____	_____
14. _____	_____
15. _____	_____
16. _____	_____

(L 25) Underline the *compound subjects* and circle the *compound predicates* in the sentences.

17. Bianca and Monroe both have the same idea.
18. Everyone loves a circus and wants to see one.

60

19. Mr. Adams and the club will show the circus in the neighbor-hood.
20. Mr. Adams smiles and laughs.

(L 26) One verb in each sentence is incorrect. Write the *correct form of the verb* on the line.

21. "No one have seen my circus for a long time," he said.
22. "I is afraid of people after all these years."
23. "You gives your show for us," says Bianca.
24. Mr. Adams think for a minute and then agrees.
25. The club members spreads the word.
26. The circus are coming to town!

21. _____   23. _____   25. _____

22. _____   24. _____   26. _____

(L 27) Rewrite these sentences as one sentence.

27. The exciting day finally arrives.
    The wonderful day arrives.

    _____

    _____

28. The great show begins in Mr. Adams' living room.
    The great show begins at 3:30.

    _____

    _____

29. Everyone claps loudly.
    Everyone claps steadily.

    _____

    _____

30 Test

(L 16)   Circle *two adjectives* in each sentence.

1. The soft floor of the forest was covered with green moss.
2. The red bridge had a yellow roof.
3. The two children ran through the quiet meadow.
4. Young Maria loved the green hills.
5. A large black hawk flew above them.

(L 17, 18)   Write the correct form of the *adjective*.

6. It is the (beautiful) day of the year.
7. "It is (hot) than yesterday," said Maria.
8. Maria is a (fast) walker than Stanley.
9. "I would feel much (happy) if I didn't have to go home tomorrow," said Stanley.
10. "It has been the (wonderful) summer ever," said Maria.
11. "I only wish it was (long)."

6. _____   9. _____

7. _____   10. _____

8. _____   11. _____

(L 19)   Circle the *adverb* in each sentence.

12. Stanley climbed slowly onto the dusty bus.
13. Maria waved sadly.
14. "Visit me soon, Maria," he said.
15. "And write to me tonight!"
16. "I will really miss you."
17. The bus rolled away.

(L 20)   Circle the group of words in each sentence that tells *where, when,* or *how*.

18. The bus roared down the road.
19. Stanley fell asleep at 5 P.M.
20. He woke up with a start.
21. No one else was in the bus.
22. He saw people running through the bus station.
23. "Wake up, Sonny," the driver said. "You're in New York."

(L 23) End each sentence with a *period*, a *question mark*, or an *exclamation point*.

    24. Did I fall asleep _____
    25. I guess I did _____
    26. Wow! That was the shortest trip ever _____
    27. What should I do now _____
    28. I'll go home and go to sleep _____

(L 24) Draw one line under the *simple subject* of each sentence. Draw two lines under the *simple predicate*.

    29. The boy walked down the hot streets.
    30. A subway rumbled beneath his feet.
    31. A jet streaked across the purple sky.
    32. Twelve pigeons sat on a bench.
    33. They fluttered away in the wind.

(L 25) Draw a circle around the *compound subject* or the *compound predicate* in each sentence.

    34. A man and a woman walked past Stanley.
    35. They smiled and laughed.
    36. Stanley sang and whistled softly.
    37. The streets and sidewalks were filled with people.
    38. Music and sounds filled the air.

(L 26) Write the correct *simple predicate* for each sentence.

    39. In a few minutes, Stanley (reaches, reach) his building.
    40. He (takes, take) the elevator to the twenty-first floor.
    41. His parents (asks, ask) him about his trip.
    42. They (listens, listen) carefully to his stories.
    43. Stanley is still tired; he (goes, go) right to bed.
    44. Soon he (dreams, dream) about a covered bridge and a river far away.

39. _____   41. _____   43. _____

40. _____   42. _____   44. _____

Try It

Draw a line under the *series* of words in this sentence.

I want a bacon, lettuce, and tomato sandwich.

☐ First Check: Did you underline *bacon, lettuce, and tomato*?

RULE: A list of three or more words, or groups of words, in a *sentence* is a *series*.

Tom, Dick, and Harry make the finest sandwiches in town.

Draw a line under the *series* in each sentence.

1. Their lunch wagon is only a hop, skip, and a jump away.
2. I'm so hungry I could buy, borrow, or beg one of Tom's pies.
3. My three favorite pies are apple, cherry, and pecan.

Sometimes each part of a *series* is a group of words. Draw lines under the series in these sentences.

4. Tom bakes cakes, makes shakes, and cooks steaks.
5. Dick breaks dishes, makes silly wishes, and cleans the fish.
6. Harry tells jokes, hums songs, and laughs often.
7. Working hard, playing games, and telling stories are part of the job.

Finish each *series* with a group of words.

8. Harry combs his hair, straightens his tie, and _____

_____

9. Dick puts a dime in the phone, dials a number, and _____

_____

Combine this group of sentences by writing one sentence with a *series*.

10. Harry wrings his hands. Harry pulls his hair. Harry worries about

business. _____

_____

RULE: Use a *comma* to separate each word or group of words listed in a series. Do not use a comma after the last word of a series.

Lisa Marie, Betty Louise, Sue Ellen, and Ashaki ate lunch together.

Fix It Read the sentence below. How many girls are eating lunch now?

Lisa, Marie, Betty Louise, Sue, Ellen, and Ashaki ate lunch.

☐ Second Check: Did you count four girls in the rule sentence and six girls in the sentence above?

Place a *comma* after each item in a series. Then tell how many items are in each series.

11. "We had warm milk dry sandwiches and cookies." _____
12. "Salad turkey juice and fruit would taste better," said Stan. _____
13. "I wish we could eat lunch at Tom Dick and Harry's." _____
14. "There is too much noise steam and movement in the school lunchroom," Ellen added. _____

Fix It The students weren't happy with this menu:

fruit juice, turkey soup, ice cream cake, and milk

"I'd like a piece of fruit," said Ashaki.
"I'd like some turkey slices," said Betty Louise.
"I'd like two different desserts," said Sly.

15. Can you add three *commas* to the menu so that each student gets what he or she wants? Do not add any more words. Write the new menu on the lines.

_____

_____

Write It Write a short paragraph about what you eat for lunch. Tell about where you eat lunch, too. Write at least three sentences that have a series of words in them.

Try It

Place a *comma* in each of the following sentences.

Tom, Dick, and Harry's Lunch Wagon opened on January 1 1980. Now they make the finest food in Cincinnati Ohio.

☐   First Check: Did you place a comma after *January 1*? Did you place a comma after *Cincinnati*?

RULE: **When writing a date that includes the *year*, place a *comma between* the day and the year.**

Tom, Dick, and Harry had their first pie-eating contest on July 4, 1980.

If the date does *not* end the sentence, place a *comma after the year*, too.

On July 4, 1981, they will have a cake-baking contest.

When writing a *city* and *state*, place a *comma between* the name of the *city* and *state*.

The blueberries for their pies come from Seattle, Washington.

If the name of the state does *not* end the sentence, place a *comma after the state*.

Farmers in Peacock, Georgia, grow the pecans for Tom's pecan pies.

Add *commas* to these sentences.

1. Tom Mayo was born in Columbus Ohio.
2. May 23 1946 was his birthdate.
3. Dick Harbarger arrived in Cincinnati on February 2 1976.
4. He used to broil steaks and fry trout in Denver Colorado.
5. Harry Heck is from Ontario Canada.
6. From May 11 1970 to April 5 1974 Harry made his own ice cream at Frozen Lake Montana.
7. Since June 1 1978 he has run the ice cream counter at Tom Dick and Harry's lunch wagon in Cincinnati Ohio.
8. People from as far away as Augusta Maine and San Diego California say Harry's ice cream is the best in the country.
9. On July 4 1980 Tom Dick and Harry will have a pie-eating contest.

RULE: When a sentence starts with an introductory word, or a person's name, there is a *pause* or short stop after that word. A comma should be written after the word to show the pause.

Yes, I'm going to the pie-eating contest.
Ashaki, I thought you were on a diet!

If a sentence ends with the name of a person being spoken to, place a comma before the name.

Don't worry about my diet, Stan.

Add *commas* where they belong in these sentences.

10. Ashaki wasn't Sly born on July 4 1968?
11. Yes I think he was. So what?
12. Well don't you see? His birthday is the day of the contest.
13. Hmmm at least we won't have to bake him a cake.
14. Stan does Sly know about the contest?
15. What did you say Lisa Marie?
16. Does Sly know about the contest Stan?
17. Of course he persuaded Tom to have it in the first place, and on his birthday Lisa Marie.
18. July 4 1980 dawned bright and clear.
19. Cincinnati Ohio was the place.
20. Lisa Marie you were away on the Fourth of July.
21. Did Sly look like he was hungry Stan?
22. No he just looked like Sly.
23. Was he ahead from the start Ashaki?
24. Yes and by noon there were just three people left.
25. There was Sly a woman from Muncie Indiana and a man who looked like he hadn't eaten since July 4 1976.
26. Sly finally won when he ate his eleventh pie Lisa Marie.
27. Yes he then ate one more for good luck.
28. After all it was his twelfth birthday Lisa Marie.

Write It   Write a short paragraph about your favorite food. Tell why you like it and how you like it prepared.

Try It

The following sentence needs *quotation marks*. Write them where they belong.

Let's have a picnic, said Ashaki.

☐   First Check: Did you put quotation marks before *Let's* and after *picnic*?

RULE: The *exact words* of the speaker should be enclosed in *quotation marks*. The speaker's first word begins with a capital letter.

"How about this Saturday?" asked Betty Louise.
Sue Ellen said, "That's fine with me."

In these sentences, place *quotation marks* where they belong.

1. Who should we invite? asked Sue Ellen.
2. I don't know, Sue Ellen. I guess everyone, answered Stan.
3. Even Sly? asked Sue Ellen.
4. Of course, he's my best friend, answered Ashaki.
5. He eats as much as three normal people! she complained.
6. That's true, but he's more fun than any three people I know, said Ashaki.
7. Anyway, picnics are for eating, she continued.

RULE: A *dialogue tag* tells who is speaking. Use a *comma* to separate the *dialogue tag* from the words being spoken.

"Let's eat by the pond," *said Sue Ellen.*
Ashaki answered, "That would be great."

A comma is not added if what is said needs a question mark or exclamation point.

"Let's eat now!" Sly shouted.
"When was the last time you ate?" asked Sue Ellen.

Sometimes a *dialogue tag* comes between two parts of a quotation.

"I had two breakfasts," he said, "and an early lunch."

Quotation Marks

Place *commas* and *quotation marks* where they belong in the following sentences.

8. The sandwiches look great said Sly. I'd like a few now.
9. Thanks we knew you'd like them said Sue Ellen.
10. No chocolate-covered bumblebees? asked Sly.
11. Chocolate-covered what? asked Ashaki. What's wrong with you, Sly?
12. Nothing. I'm just a nature lover said Sly.

RULE: **In a written conversation, a new *paragraph* begins each time the speaker changes. This makes it easier to understand who is speaking.**

   "Do you see what I see?" asked Lisa Marie as she looked at the ground behind Stan.
   "You mean millions and millions of ants?" said Ashaki.
   "Yes, millions and millions of ants," said Stan. "And they're all coming this way!"

Fix It   Rewrite the following conversation. Add *quotation marks*. Start a *new paragraph* each time the speaker changes.

Let's get out of here! shouted Stan. They're only ants, so let's keep eating, said Sly. If we had some chocolate, we could just cover them all, offered Sue Ellen. Are you crazy? asked Ashaki. No, just hungry, they both answered.

_____

_____

_____

_____

_____

_____

Write It   Write a conversation between two people who are arguing. Remember to start a new paragraph each time the speaker changes.

Try It

Place *commas* where they belong in this letter.

October 30 1980

Dear Lisa Marie

    Last night I dreamt my swimming pool was filled with root beer. I was floating on a giant ice cream sandwich. You kept nibbling on the ice cream raft until it was gone. Then I fell into the root beer. I almost drowned! Thanks a lot!

Yours truly
Sly

☐   First Check: Did you place a *comma after the day* and *before the year* in the date? Did you place commas after *Lisa Marie* and *truly*?

RULE: **A friendly letter has five parts: the *date*, the *greeting*, the *body*, the *closing*, and the *signature*.**

November 2, 1980   (DATE)

Dear Sly,   (GREETING)

    I am not responsible for what I do in your dreams. Anyway, after I ate all that ice cream, I'm sure I would have drunk the root beer, too. So there was nothing to worry about.   (BODY)

Your friend,   (CLOSING)
Lisa Marie   (SIGNATURE)

The following letter is missing *commas*. Place commas where they belong.

November 4 1980

Dear Lisa Marie

    You did it again! I dreamt I was hiding from a monster behind a shelf of cookies at the supermarket. You came along and started eating cookies. You ate the chocolate the oatmeal and the lemon sandwich cookies. By then the monster could see me. I had to wake up to get away from him.

Your worried friend
Sly

☐ Second Check: Did you find a series in the letter? Did you add commas where they belong?

Fix It

The five parts of this letter are not in the right place. *Rewrite* the letter correctly.

Lisa Marie

Sincerely yours,

   I was sorry to hear about your run-in with the monster. Yes, I have always liked lemon sandwich cookies. Perhaps I have liked them too much. I am sorry for all the trouble I have caused.

Dear Sly

November 19 1980

_____

_____

_____

_____

_____

_____

_____

_____

_____

Write It

Pretend you are Lisa Marie. Write another letter to Sly. Tell him about a dream you have had.

Try It

Add *commas* to these sentences.

"On July 14 1982 a very strange thing happened at my house in Cincinnati Ohio."

"Sue Ellen you had a good time though" said Stan.

"Yes but I was upset when all those pizzas hamburgers chickens and desserts started to arrive at my door" she said.

☐ First Check: Did you add 10 *commas*?

> **RULE: Always use *commas*:**
> **Between the name of a city and a state:** Lima, Ohio
> **Between the day of the month and the year:** June 30, 1776
> **Between words in a series:** scrambled eggs, poached eggs, and fried eggs
> **After the greeting and closing of a friendly letter:** Dear Sly, Yours truly,
> **To set off the names of persons spoken to:** Sue Ellen, your pizza is here.
> **To set off introductory words at the beginning of a sentence:** No, I didn't order a pizza.
> **To separate the words of a speaker from a dialogue tag:** "I said I didn't order the pizzas," she repeated.

1. Read the following paragraphs. Add *commas* wherever they are needed.

The pizzas were from the Pizza Palace in Ebony Ohio. They were covered with mushrooms tomatoes extra cheese and pepperoni.

"Yes I'm sure this is the right address" the delivery girl said "and the right date—July 14 1982."

Then the doorbell rang again.

"Sue Ellen Harrison I have your orders of fried chicken" the delivery man said.

"Chicken? I never ordered chicken" the confused girl explained.

The bell rang again and again and again. Delivery people were bringing sandwiches ice cream soft drinks and cakes.

"No I don't know what's happening Mother" Sue Ellen said.

☐ Second Check: Did you add 16 commas?

Use It

The words *isn't* and *aren't* are contractions that mean *is not* and *are not*.

Use *isn't* with a singular subject.

"If this is a joke, it *isn't* very funny," said Mrs. Harrison.

Use *aren't* with a plural subject. Use *aren't* with *you*.

The Harrisons *aren't* able to understand what is happening.

"You *aren't* going to eat all this food, are you, Sue Ellen?"

Complete each sentence with *isn't* or *aren't*.

2. "We ___ going to pay for this food," said Mrs. Harrison.
3. "It ___ fair; we didn't even order it."
4. "___ you at least going to pay for the pizza you're eating?" the delivery girl asked.
5. "This ice cream is melting. My bosses ___ going to like this," one man complained.
6. "___ that Sly Greene with Stan, Lisa Marie, and the others across the street?"
7. They ___ here by accident, I bet."

2. _____   4. _____   6. _____

3. _____   5. _____   7. _____

> **RULE:** When a *quotation* comes at the end of a sentence, the period, the question mark, or the exclamation point is written *inside* the quotation marks.
>
> Sue Ellen shouted, "Hello, Sly, how are you?"
> Sly said, "I feel fine."
> The whole gang shouted, "Happy Un-Birthday, Sue Ellen!"

Complete each sentence with a *period, question mark*, or *exclamation point* and *quotation marks*.

8. Sue Ellen asked, "What's an Un-Birthday _____
9. Stan replied, "It's an excuse for a party _____
10. "That's right," shouted Sly, "and a chance to do some serious eating _____
11. "Because we like you," said Stan, "and because we love pizza, chicken, hamburgers, and ice cream _____

Write It   Write a paragraph in which you describe a conversation about the food at a party. Use quotation marks.

Write four sentences about food. Each sentence should have a *series* of words. Remember to put *commas* where they belong.

1. _____

2. _____

3. _____

4. _____

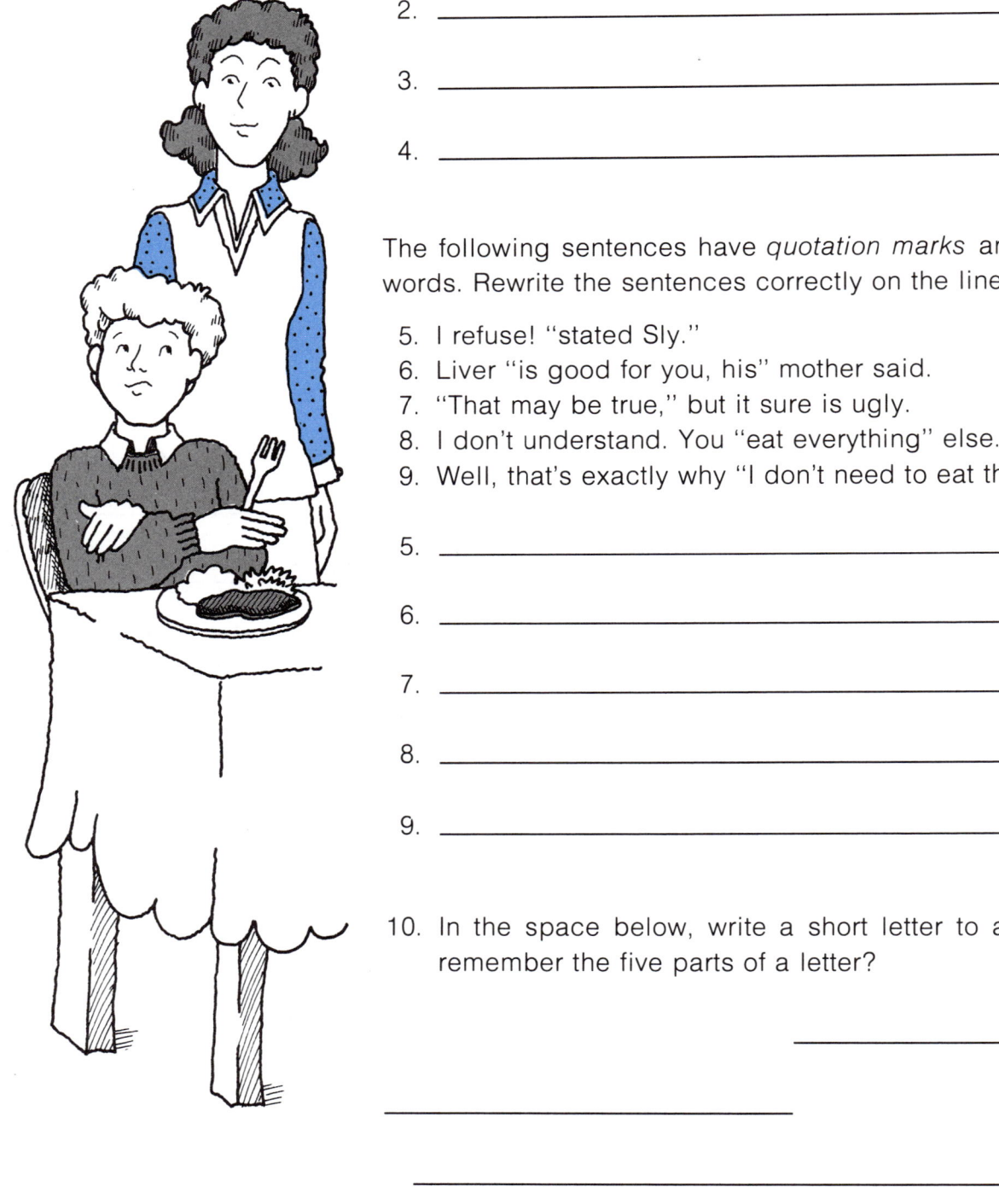

The following sentences have *quotation marks* around the wrong words. Rewrite the sentences correctly on the lines.

5. I refuse! "stated Sly."
6. Liver "is good for you, his" mother said.
7. "That may be true," but it sure is ugly.
8. I don't understand. You "eat everything" else.
9. Well, that's exactly why "I don't need to eat this!"

5. _____

6. _____

7. _____

8. _____

9. _____

10. In the space below, write a short letter to a friend. Do you remember the five parts of a letter?

_____

_____

_____

_____

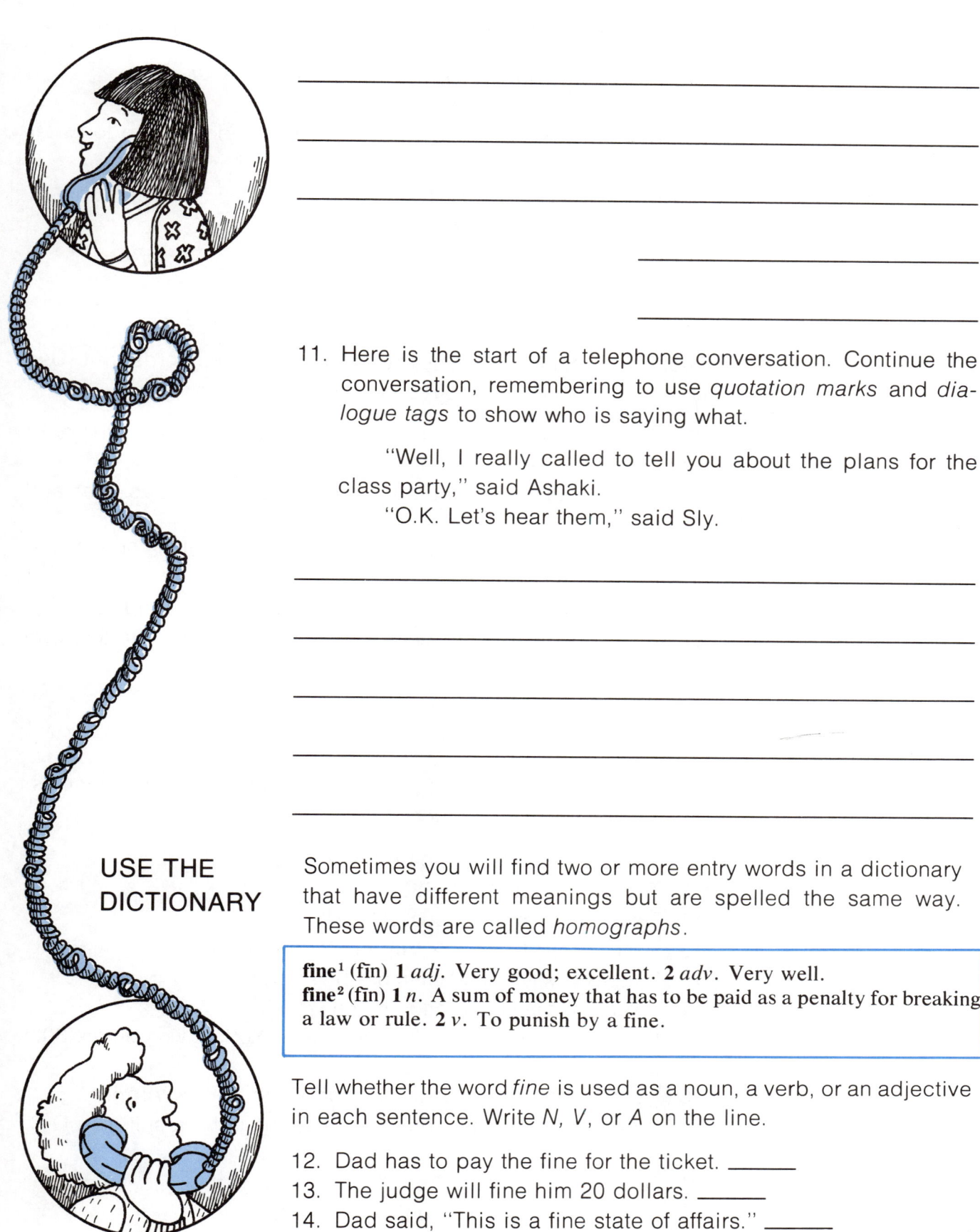

_____

_____

_____

_____

_____

11. Here is the start of a telephone conversation. Continue the conversation, remembering to use *quotation marks* and *dialogue tags* to show who is saying what.

"Well, I really called to tell you about the plans for the class party," said Ashaki.
"O.K. Let's hear them," said Sly.

_____

_____

_____

_____

_____

USE THE DICTIONARY

Sometimes you will find two or more entry words in a dictionary that have different meanings but are spelled the same way. These words are called *homographs*.

> **fine**¹ (fīn) **1** *adj.* Very good; excellent. **2** *adv.* Very well.
> **fine**² (fīn) **1** *n.* A sum of money that has to be paid as a penalty for breaking a law or rule. **2** *v.* To punish by a fine.

Tell whether the word *fine* is used as a noun, a verb, or an adjective in each sentence. Write *N, V,* or *A* on the line.

12. Dad has to pay the fine for the ticket. _____
13. The judge will fine him 20 dollars. _____
14. Dad said, "This is a fine state of affairs." _____

37 Review

(L 35)   Complete each sentence by adding the correct punctuation mark.

1. Do you like going out to restaurants for dinner _____
2. We don't do it very often _____
3. There's one reason why I really like it! I don't have to wash any of the dishes _____
4. The food isn't always that good _____
5. Sometimes it's really great _____
6. Often I wonder, "What am I eating _____"

(L 31)   Each of the following sentences has a *series* of words in it. Use *commas* to punctuate them properly.

7. We ate breakfast at home lunch at a small place by the road and dinner in a hotel.
8. For breakfast we had orange juice toast milk strawberries and melon.
9. For lunch I had a chicken salad sandwich a glass of milk and a piece of apple pie.
10. Dinner was great: pea soup fried chicken and a big salad.
11. When I finally went to sleep that night I was dirty tired and very full.

(L 32)   Each of the following sentences is missing one or two *commas*. Write them where they belong.

12. We left Cincinnati Ohio on Wednesday.
13. That was August 18 1980.
14. Dad was born on August 22 1942.
15. We're going to Norfolk Virginia for his birthday.
16. "Dad will we reach Baltimore by Friday?"
17. "Well if it doesn't rain too much we will."
18. Dad said that the last time he was in Norfolk was on his 30th birthday, August 24 1972.
19. He was born right outside of Norfolk, in Suffolk Virginia.
20. After we got to Baltimore, we drove through Washington D.C. and into Virginia.
21. "Dad are we almost there?"
22. "Yes Sue Ellen we'll be there by eight o'clock."

(L 33)   Put *quotation marks* where they are needed in these sentences.

23. It sounds like you don't enjoy the driving very much, Sue Ellen's father said.
24. It's not bad, but it makes me very hungry.
25. A lot of things seem to make you hungry, Dad complained.
26. Are you saying that I eat too much? she asked.
27. No, he replied, not at all.
28. Then he added, I like to eat as much as you do.
29. Well, since we all like to eat so much, let's stop.
30. Right now? Can't you wait until we get to Norfolk? Mr. Harrison asked.
31. You see. I knew it. You do think I eat too much.
32. No. I just think it would be nice to eat in Norfolk.
33. O.K. You're forgiven, she said finally.

(L 33, L 35)   The following conversation is missing *quotation marks* and *commas*. Punctuation is needed to separate the dialogue tags from what is being said. Put the missing marks where they belong.

34. Where are we going to go for dinner? asked Sue Ellen.
35. What do you feel like eating?
36. A lot she answered.
37. No, I want a serious answer.
38. Well, how about a health food place? she said.
39. That's fine with me her father answered.
40. You don't look too happy about it.
41. I guess I had something more filling in mind he said.
42. Dad, you're just asking to get fat said Sue Ellen.
43. I take care of myself, he replied.
44. Then he added Wait a minute, are you saying that I eat too much?
45. Oh come on, Dad, would I say something like that?
46. You certainly would he answered.

Try It

Can you *combine* these two sentences into one sentence? Write your sentence on the line.

She ran fast.   She won the race.

_____

☐ First Check: Did you join the two sentences with the word *and*?

RULE: **Some sentences are made up of two or more complete sentences that have been joined together. These sentences are called *compound sentences*. Each of the joined parts has its own subject and verb. The parts can be joined by *and, but, or*, or a semicolon (;). If you use *and, but*, or *or*, put a comma before it.**

She ran fast, *and* she won the race.
He ran fast, *but* someone else won.
Did she win, *or* did her friend win?
She won; her friend came in second.

Look at each sentence. Decide if it is a *compound sentence* or a *simple sentence*. If it is a simple sentence, write *S* on the line. If it is a compound sentence, underline both subjects and both verbs. Circle the word that *joins* the sentences.

_____ 1. Wyomia Tyus was a famous runner, and she was the fastest woman of the 1960s.
_____ 2. She won the 100-meter race in two Olympics in a row.
_____ 3. She raced against fine runners like Irena Szewinska.
_____ 4. Irena Szewinska is one of the best runners of all.
_____ 5. Irena Szewinska has run in four Olympic Games, and she has won medals in each of them.
_____ 6. She has won short races such as the 200-meter race; she has won longer races, too.
_____ 7. Good runners have to practice very hard, or they do not win often.

Rewrite each pair of simple sentences. Join them to make one *compound sentence*. Use *and, but, or*, or a *;*. Sometimes several conjunctions will fit into the sentence. Choose the one that fits the best.

8. Jim Thorpe won two events in the 1912 Olympics. He was called the greatest athlete of his time.

_____

_____

9. Thorpe would try almost any kind of sport. He won at most of them.

_____

_____

10. He was the finest football player at the Carlisle Indian School. He was also good at running, jumping, and throwing sports.

_____

_____

11. Now most of his records have been broken. Few people since Thorpe have been as good at so many things at once.

_____

_____

Write It

Write three sentences about sports, games, or players you know about. You can talk about sports you enjoy doing. Use one conjunction or a *;* in each sentence.

39 Modifying Phrases

Try It

Look at the sentence. Underline the *word group* that describes the singer.

Tonight I heard a singer with great talent.

☐ First Check: Did you underline the words *with great talent*?

RULE: **A *phrase* is a group of words that goes together. A phrase does not have a subject and a verb. It cannot stand alone as a sentence. All the words in the phrase have the same purpose. They tell *when, where, how, what kind*, or *to whom*. One common kind of phrase begins with a word like *of, to*, or *from*. Words like these are called *prepositions*. Here are some other prepositions:**

behind   with   on   under   around   in   for   through

Circle the *phrase* in each sentence. Then write the phrase on the line.

1. Charley Pride was born in Mississippi.
2. He lived with his 10 brothers and sisters.
3. He worked in the cotton fields.
4. He bought a guitar for 10 dollars.
5. Charley Pride bought it through the mail.
6. He began playing songs on his guitar.

1. _____   4. _____

2. _____   5. _____

3. _____   6. _____

RULE: **Some prepositional phrases describe *people*, *places*, or *things*. These phrases are called *adjective phrases*.**

Charley Pride owned a guitar *with six strings*.

Adverbial phrases tell *where, when*, or *how* an action occurs.

He bought the guitar *in another town*.

Underline the *phrase* in each sentence.

7. Charley Pride is a man with a fine voice.
8. A radio show in Charley's town asked him to sing.
9. He did so in 1963.
10. Listeners thought that he sang with great talent.
11. People said he belonged in Nashville, Tennessee.
12. Nashville is the center of country music.
13. Charley packed his bags and went to Nashville.
14. There Charley had much success in his career.

Use It The forms of the verb *break* sometimes cause confusion. The past form of *break* is *broke*. Never use a helping verb with *broke*.

Last week Charley broke his guitar.

The verb form *broken* is always used with a helping verb.

Charley *has broken* the guitar.

Complete these sentences. Write *broke* or *broken* on the lines.

15. The boy ___ the music stand by accident.
16. It was ___ once before.
17. The other music stand is ___, too.
18. Can you fix wooden things that are ___?
19. Nobody ___ the piano.
20. It ___ by itself.

15. _____   17. _____   19. _____

16. _____   18. _____   20. _____

Write It Write three sentences using *prepositional phrases*. Choose your phrases from this list.

in a blue dress   in the corner   without windows
with brown hair   with a long tail   of brown wood

Try It

Look at this sentence. Its subject is *doctors*; its verb is *practiced*. There is another subject and verb in the sentence. Underline the other subject and verb.

Before Elizabeth Blackwell studied medicine, no women doctors practiced in America.

☐ First Check: Did you underline *Elizabeth Blackwell* and *studied*?

RULE: **A *clause* is a word group within a sentence. A clause has its own subject and verb. Many clauses begin with the words *before, since, after, while, if, where, because,* or *although*. These clauses *cannot* stand alone as complete sentences.**

When she went to New York City, Elizabeth Blackwell started a hospital.
When she went to New York City, (clause)
Elizabeth Blackwell started a hospital. (complete sentence)

Circle the *clause* in each sentence. Then write the word that begins the clause on the line.

1. When Elizabeth Blackwell was young, she had a very good education.
2. Although few girls were well-educated then, Elizabeth's father felt that women should have the same opportunities as men.
3. After Elizabeth taught school, she set out to become a doctor.
4. Because she was a woman, no medical school would accept her.
5. After many schools refused her, she finally got into Geneva Medical College in New York State.
6. Although many people were unhappy about this, Elizabeth kept studying.
7. When she completed her studies, she became Dr. Blackwell.
8. Although she was now an M.D., no hospital would employ her.
9. After several years of further study in Europe, Dr. Blackwell returned to the United States.
10. When she returned to this country, she settled in New York.
11. Because she did such good work, people began to accept the idea of women doctors.

12. After Blackwell got her M.D., other women were able to study medicine.

1. _____   5. _____   9. _____

2. _____   6. _____   10. _____

3. _____   7. _____   11. _____

4. _____   8. _____   12. _____

Draw lines to match each *clause* in column A with a *sentence* in column B.

Column A

13. When Dr. Blackwell gave talks to women's groups,
14. After Elizabeth's sister, Emily, also became a doctor,
15. When Elizabeth Blackwell started a women's medical college,

Column B

It was the first such school in the United States.

Many women learned health care for the first time.

Emily was able to help Elizabeth in her work.

Combine each pair of word groups into one sentence.

16. when Elizabeth Blackwell first came to New York City
    no patients would come to her

_____

_____

_____

17. after women went to her health classes
    they began to believe in her

_____

_____

_____

Try It

This sentence tells the main idea of the paragraph.

> Many people believe that everyone should speak the same language.

Which of these sentences belong in the paragraph? Put an X next to each sentence that belongs.

_____ a. With a single language we could all understand one another.

_____ b. Some people never learn to write.

_____ c. That is why Ludwig Zamenhof invented Esperanto in 1917.

_____ d. Zamenhof wanted a language that everyone could learn.

☐ First Check: Did you check *a, c,* and *d*?

RULE: A *paragraph* is a group of sentences about the same subject.

Read each numbered sentence. It begins a *paragraph*. Put an X next to each lettered sentence that belongs in the paragraph.

1. Sequoya was a Cherokee who invented a form of writing for his people.

_____ a. Before the 1820s, the native people of North America had no way of writing their languages.

_____ b. The Chinese have used paper for hundreds of years.

_____ c. Sequoya decided on 85 "letters" for the different sounds of the Cherokee language.

_____ d. By 1828 the Bible, the Cherokee laws, and a Cherokee newspaper had been printed in Cherokee.

2. For hundreds of years, people had to write every book by hand.

_____ a. Many people like to read comics.

_____ b. Then in the 1430s Johann Gutenberg of Germany developed a printing press with movable type.

_____ c. He was the first European to find a way to print books.

_____ d. People could produce many copies of the same book quickly.

84

RULE: **The sentences in a paragraph should follow each other in some kind of order. The order in which things happen in time is one kind of order.**

As a child Noah Webster was interested in books. As a young man he taught school. He also wrote spelling books. When he grew older, he wrote the first American dictionary.

Fix It

Each paragraph below is mixed up. On the line, write the sentence that should begin the paragraph.

3. Later he perfected an alphabet of raised dots. He went to a special school for the blind. He lost his sight as a young child. Louis Braille was born in France in 1809. Blind people could "read" this alphabet with their fingers.

_____

4. In 1670, he invented semaphores. King James II of England was born in 1633. The sender waves two flags in different directions. Someone standing far away can easily see what the sender is saying. This is a way of sending messages.

_____

Use It

The words *this, that, these,* and *those* are hard-working words in our language. They can come before a noun, or they can stand alone like pronouns. *This* and *that* tell about one person, place, or thing. *These* and *those* tell about more than one.

I own *this* book.   *That* language is difficult.
I like *this* very much.   I heard *that*!

Circle the word that completes each sentence correctly.

5. (This, These) language uses a different alphabet from ours.
6. It is spoken by people from (that, those) country.
7. I learned it from (that, those) people.
8. (This, These) books will teach you how to read the language.

Write It

Choose one sentence from the list. Use it as the first sentence of a paragraph. Write a short paragraph.

There are many languages in the world.
I would like to know another language.
I know several people who speak more than one language.

42 Topic Sentences

Try It

Read this paragraph. Which sentence tells the *main idea* of the paragraph? Underline that sentence.

> Writers tell many kinds of stories. Some writers tell about nature and animals. Some tell about people. Others retell stories that are hundreds of years old. Still others make up people and places that could never be found in the real world.

☐ First Check: Did you underline the first sentence?

RULE: A *topic sentence* tells the main idea of a paragraph. The topic sentence is often the first sentence in the paragraph. It can also be written later in the paragraph.

Underline the *topic sentence* in each of these paragraphs.

1. Some of Tom and Muriel Feelings' books are about black neighborhoods in cities. Other books show people in different African countries. Mr. and Mrs. Feelings have even written a book called *Maja Means One*. It is about counting in Swahili, an African language. Books by Tom and Muriel Feelings describe what life is like for black people around the world.

2. Kazue Mizumura spent most of her early life in Japan. She was born there. She spent her childhood there during World War II. She later went to a Japanese art school. She did not come to the United States until she was a grown woman. In the United States she wrote and illustrated such books as *The Emperor Penguins*.

3. Many people who now write in English first spoke another language. Eva-Lis Wuorio (*Return of the Viking*) first spoke Finnish. Isaac B. Singer spoke Yiddish, a language of European Jews. Victor Ambrus (*The Sultan's Bath*) spoke Hungarian when he was growing up.

Choose the best *topic sentence* for each of these paragraphs. Write the topic sentence on the line. Remember to indent your sentence if it is the first sentence in the paragraph.

4. _____

_____ She and her brothers made

up hundreds of stories for one another. They also put on plays they wrote themselves. Later Mary Norton wrote whole books full of her stories. Books such as *The Borrowers* brought her stories to all children.

A. From childhood Mary Norton liked making up stories.
B. Mary Norton had four brothers.

5. Isaac Bashevis Singer wrote *The Family Moskat* and *In My Father's Court* for adults. He wrote *Why Noah Chose the Dove* and *Joseph and Koza* for children. _____

_____

A. Singer is a writer that people of all ages enjoy.
B. Singer has traveled to many parts of the world.

6. _____

_____ Sidney Taylor's *All-of-a-Kind Family* is based on her childhood in New York City. The *Little House* books by Laura Ingalls Wilder tell about her life on the prairie in the 1800s. Louisa May Alcott's *Little Women* is about her growing up in New England in the 1800s.

A. Sidney Taylor's books have been read by many people.
B. Many writers use their own lives for their stories.

Write It

Write a paragraph about a writer or book you like. Be sure to write a topic sentence in your paragraph. Underline your topic sentence.

_____

_____

_____

_____

_____

_____

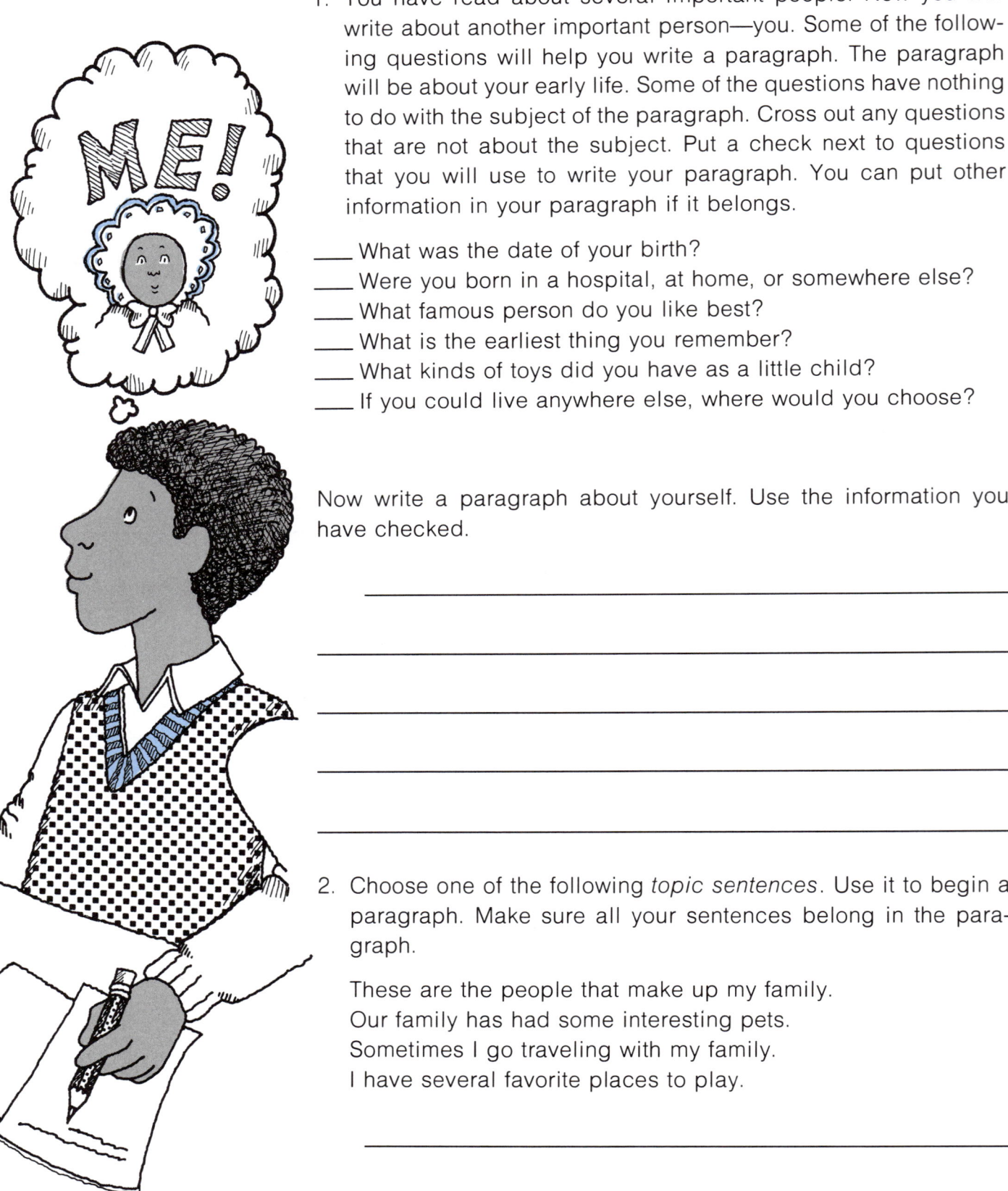

1. You have read about several important people. Now you will write about another important person—you. Some of the following questions will help you write a paragraph. The paragraph will be about your early life. Some of the questions have nothing to do with the subject of the paragraph. Cross out any questions that are not about the subject. Put a check next to questions that you will use to write your paragraph. You can put other information in your paragraph if it belongs.

____ What was the date of your birth?
____ Were you born in a hospital, at home, or somewhere else?
____ What famous person do you like best?
____ What is the earliest thing you remember?
____ What kinds of toys did you have as a little child?
____ If you could live anywhere else, where would you choose?

Now write a paragraph about yourself. Use the information you have checked.

_____

_____

_____

_____

_____

2. Choose one of the following *topic sentences*. Use it to begin a paragraph. Make sure all your sentences belong in the paragraph.

These are the people that make up my family.
Our family has had some interesting pets.
Sometimes I go traveling with my family.
I have several favorite places to play.

_____

_____

_____

_____

_____

_____

3. Write a paragraph that tells about the past two years of your life. Put the events you tell about in the right order.

_____

_____

_____

_____

_____

_____

USE THE DICTIONARY

A *suffix* is one or more syllables added to the end of a word to make another word. Some suffixes are entries in the dictionary. Read the definitions of these common suffixes.

-ful—full of; able to	**-less**—without; not having
-fy—to make or cause to be	**-ly**—in a certain manner

Look at the words. Think about what each word means. Circle the suffix in each word. Then write the word that the suffix was added to.

4. beautify _____   8. certainly _____

5. penniless _____   9. glorify _____

6 plentiful _____   10. cupful _____

7. helpless _____   11. happily _____

(L 38) Make each pair of sentences into one *compound sentence*. Join them together with *and, but,* or *or*.

1. Maria Tallchief was born in Fairfax, Oklahoma. She lived there

   as a small child. _____

   _____

2. Her grandfather had been a chief of the Osage Indians. Maria

   was a member of the tribe, too. _____

   _____

3. She watched the tribal dances of her people. At the age of four

   she began to study ballet. _____

   _____

4. Maria enjoyed ballet dancing. She also learned how to play

   the piano. _____

   _____

5. She knew she could spend her life dancing. She could be a

   fine piano player. _____

   _____

Underline the *phrases* in these sentences.

6. Maria Tallchief was a clever girl with great talent.
7. She once gave a dance show for her friends.
8. Many books on ballet have pictures of Maria.
9. The pictures show Maria in beautiful costumes.
10. Maria Tallchief was one of the finest dancers in the world.

(L 39) Write the *clause* in each sentence.

11. When Maria was eight, her family moved to Los Angeles,

California. _____

12. Because Los Angeles had better dancing teachers, the family

moved there. _____

13. Because Maria was good at both music and dance, she could

not choose between them. _____

14. When she was 16, she decided on dancing as a career.

_____

(L 41) 15. Which sentences belong in this paragraph? Look at the topic
sentence. Then choose the sentences from the list that belong.
Put an X next to those sentences. Write them in the paragraph.

Maria Tallchief has danced in many cities and countries.

_____

_____

_____

_____

____ She first danced in public in Hollywood, California.
____ She was unusually tall for a dancer.
____ When she was 17, she took a dancing job in New York City.
____ With her ballet company, she traveled to other American cities.
____ She also danced in European countries, like Britain.
____ Her sister Marjorie was also a dancer.

(L 42) 16. Which sentence would be a good *topic sentence* for a paragraph on how a dancer prepares? Underline that sentence.

a. A tall dancer looks better in dark outfits.
b. A dancer must work hard every day to prepare for a show.
c. Some dancers are stronger than others.

45 Test

(L 31) Draw a line under the *series* in each sentence. Add *commas* where necessary.

1. My father has worked as a musician a fisherman a truck driver an actor and a salesman.
2. As kids we lived in Kansas California Ohio and Rhode Island.
3. My father my sister and I picked apples one summer.
4. We have lived in a trailer a tent a farmhouse and a high-rise apartment.
5. Cities suburbs and mountaintops are nice places to live.

(L 32) Add *commas* where needed in these sentences.

6. On April 4 1986 we moved to Nevada.
7. Dad played the piano in a hotel in Reno Nevada.
8. We went to school there until June 23 1986.
9. Then we all worked on a ranch near Elko Nevada.
10. On April 1 1987 we moved to Little Compton Rhode Island.
11. Dad was a lobsterman for a while—until November 30 1987.

(L 33) Place *quotation marks* around the exact words of each speaker. Add *commas, periods*, and *question marks* where necessary.

12. Why did you want to be a fisherman Dad I asked
13. I've always loved the sea Richard he said
14. Of course we all like good shellfish he continued which were hard to get in Nevada
15. Why doesn't Aunt Elma want you to work with her anymore I asked
16. I'm not sure Dad said but I think we're going to have to move again

(L 34) 17. Add *commas* where necessary in this letter. Write the name of each part of the letter on the lines.

November 30 1987 _____

Dear Aunt Elma _____

   Please let my Dad work longer as a fisherman. We like your Rhode Island and lobsters.

Your nephew _____

Richard _____

92

(L 38) Underline the two *subjects* and two *predicates* in each compound sentence. Circle the *conjunction* in each sentence.

18. Well, Dad lost the job, and we left Rhode Island.
19. We could go back to Nevada, or we could move somewhere else.
20. Dad was upset, but there was nothing we could do.
21. Dad packed our things in the truck, and then we climbed in.

(L 39) Underline the *prepositional phrase* in each sentence.

22. With sad faces we drove away.
23. We knew we'd find a home in another state.
24. For two days we drove west.
25. Dad was restless; he was without a job.
26. On the third day we stopped to eat.

(L 40) Underline the *clause* in each sentence. Circle the word that begins the clause.

27. After we looked at the menu, we ordered hamburgers.
28. Since there was no ketchup on the table, Dad asked the owners for some.
29. While the owner looked for a bottle, Dad told him about the lobster business.
30. We had finished our hamburgers before Dad returned to the table.
31. "We'll be staying here for a while, kids," he said, "because I just got a job with Tom, Dick, and Harry."

(L 42) 32. Draw a line under the *topic sentence* of the paragraph. Then draw a circle around the sentence that does not belong in the paragraph.

Life in Cincinnati is great! Dad loves his work and we go to a fine school. We found a nice apartment near a large park. The beaches in Rhode Island were very nice. We are finally making some friends in our neighborhood.

Try It

To become a Space Ranger, you have to go to Ranger School. People who want to go to Ranger School fill out this form.

Name **Mayes Bonnie R.**	Date **May 1, 1998**
LAST FIRST MIDDLE INITIAL	
Address **44 Star Drive**	**July 7 1989**
STREET	Date of Birth
Phoenix Arizona 11256	Age **9**
CITY STATE ZIP	

In what year is Bonnie filling out this form? _____

☐ First Check: Did you say that she filled out the form in *1998*?

RULE: **People often have to fill out *forms*. When you fill out a form, make sure you write everything clearly and in the right place. In some forms, you must fill in your last name first.**

1. Sylvester wants to apply to Ranger School. Help him fill out his application form. His street address is 989 Palm Street. His birth date is March 9, 1980. He lives in Haiku, Hawaii. Lopaka is his last name, and 96708 is his ZIP code. Sylvester filled out the form on January 7, 1998. He is 17 years and 10 months old. His middle initial is U. He goes to Pacific School in Haiku, Hawaii.

Name _____	**Date** _____
	MONTH DAY YEAR
Address _____ . _____	
	Date of Birth
_____	
School _____	
School's Address _____	
CITY STATE ZIP	

94

2. Everyone has to take a test to get into Ranger School. If you were taking the test, you would have to fill out this heading. Fill in all the information.

```
Name _____
         LAST              FIRST                    MIDDLE INITIAL

Address _____
         NUMBER  AND  STREET

_____
CITY                      STATE                    ZIP

Age _____   Date of Birth _____
                                      MONTH     DAY      YEAR
```

Fix It

3. Brad Steele has filled in his test heading.

Name ___Brad_____Steele_____
         LAST   FIRST

What is wrong with what Brad wrote? Write the line correctly.

_____

4. Student Rangers wear special outfits. They use forms to order them. Here is some information about Chet. Use only the information you need to fill in his order form. Chet lives in Fulton, Kansas. He is $18\frac{1}{2}$ years old. His ZIP code is 66738. He is 2 m (6.5 ft.) tall. He weighs 88 kg (194 lbs.). He wears size 13 shoes. His suit size is 42 long. His street address is 45 West Avenue. His present school is Harry Truman High School. His favorite color is brown. His last name is Osceola.

```
Name _____
         FIRST                    LAST

Home Address _____
              NUMBER  AND  STREET

_____
CITY                      STATE                    ZIP

Height _____   Suit Size _____   Shoe Size _____
```

Write It

What do you think might happen at Ranger School? What equipment would you bring if you went? Write a paragraph that tells.

Try It

Bonnie Mayes has passed her test for Ranger School. She has flown to the school, which is on the moon. This map shows the Ranger School.

Bonnie must get from the sleeping quarters to the classrooms.
Here are the first two things she must do.
Walk along Venus Avenue to Starfire Road.
Turn onto Starfire Road.
What is the *next thing* she must do? Write it here.

_____

☐ First Check: Did you write that Bonnie should walk to *Night-side Street* and *turn left,* or *go west* ?

RULE: When you give *directions*, always be clear. Give each step in the right order.

Look back at the map. Give *directions* that answer each of these questions. Write the first *two* steps for each.

1. How would you walk from the rocket port to the library?

_____

_____

2. How would you get from the bridge to the park?

_____

_____

> **RULE:** **When you write a *telephone message*, make sure you write down all the necessary information.**
>
> **Name of Caller** _____ **Time** _____
> **Phone Number** _____ **Message** _____

3. How would you get from the dining hall to the gym?

_____

_____

4. At 6 A.M. Sylvester Lopaka called Captain Nash. Here is what Sylvester said to the person who answered the call. "Please tell Captain Nash that the new codes are ready for him. Ask him to call me at Code B-42X." Write the message on this form.

```
A message for _____

_____ called you at _____


(Check one) ____ He/She will call again later.
            ____ Please call him/her back at _____.

He/She also said the following: _____
```

Write It Make a map of the route you take to school. Describe this route in a paragraph.

48   Writing Invitations

Try It

A *note* is a short kind of letter. Often a note is written for a special reason. Look at this note.

October 6, 1998

Dear Captain Nash,

   The United Planets Club is having its yearly meeting on Friday, October 19. We hope you can come. The Air People from Polaris are coming for the first time. The club meets in the Ranger School Library at 8 Nightside Street. Our meeting begins at 2 P.M., Moon Time.

Sincerely,
Brad Steele

Why did Brad write this note?

_____

☐   First Check: Did you write that the note is to invite someone to a meeting?

RULE: **An *invitation* asks people to come to a party or special event. An invitation should tell these things: the kind of *event* or party, the *date* and *time*, and the *place* where it will be held.**

Event: Come to the Rocket Races
Place: The Bohr Airstrip
Time: January 12   2 P.M.

Here are the message parts of several invitations. One detail is missing from each one. Write whether the invitation needs the date, the time, the place, or the kind of event.

1. Please come to the Rangers Awards Dinner at 6 P.M. on January 7. All Student Rangers who did well in Spaceship Flying, Martian, and other studies will get prizes.

   What is missing? _____

2. Come on the class trip to Neptune! We will meet at the rocket port on Venus Avenue on May 7.

   What is missing? _____

98

3. We are having a party to welcome the Air People to the moon. Please come. It begins at 5 P.M. on May 17.

   What is missing? _____

4. Invite Bonnie Mayes to a surprise party for Chief Ranger Joan Oliver. Decide on a date and a time. Use the map on page 96 to choose a place. Write the invitation here.

   Dear Bonnie,

   _____

   _____

   _____

   _____

Use It   The verbs *let* and *leave* are often confused. They have different meanings. The verb *let* means *to allow*.

   Will you *let* me drive the spaceship?

Leave means *to go away from*.

   We will *leave* Venus in an hour.

Finish each sentence. Write *let* or *leave* on the line.

5. The ship will ___ at midnight, Venus time.
6. I do not want to ___ Venus.
7. The Rangers will ___ me come back next year.
8. Don't ___ Brad Steele and Milly Tekawitha drive!
9. They always ___ the ship go too fast.
10. They don't ___ soon enough.

5. _____   7. _____   9. _____

6. _____   8. _____   10. _____

Write It   Pretend you live in the future. Think of a future event you want to invite someone to. Write the message part of an invitation to this event.

Try It

1. HEADING		Joan Oliver, Chief Ranger Space Ranger School 200 Nightside Street Einstein City, Moon M6430 March 5, 1999
2. INSIDE ADDRESS		Angus MacBride Hotel Adonis 89 Cloud Avenue Earhart City, Venus X7943
3. GREETING		Dear Mr. MacBride:
4. BODY		The Student Rangers are planning a class trip to your planet. We would like to stay in your hotel overnight on May 7. Could you send us information on rooms and prices? There will be 12 of us. Two of the Student Rangers are from Neptune. They will need water tanks instead of beds to sleep in. Is this possible?
5. CLOSING		Sincerely,
6. SIGNATURE		Joan Oliver Chief Ranger

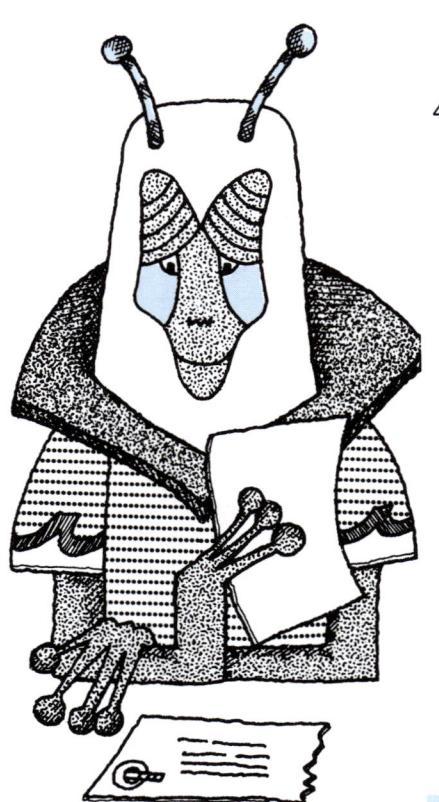

The letter above is a *business letter*. To which address is this letter being sent? _____

☐ First Check: Did you write the address of the Hotel Adonis?

RULE: A friendly letter has five parts: the heading, the greeting, the body, the closing, and the signature. A *business letter* has a sixth part—the *inside address*. This is the address of the person being written to. In a business letter, the greeting is always followed by a colon (:).

1. Finish this business letter. Mr. MacBride is writing the letter. He is writing to Chief Ranger Oliver. The date is March 10, 1999. Use information from the letter on this page. Put everything in the place it belongs. Remember that Joan Oliver will be receiving this letter.

_____

_____

_____

_____

_____

_____

_____

_____

We will be happy to have you stay at our hotel. I am sending our price list along with this letter. Please fill out the order form at the bottom of the list. We will have water tanks for the Neptunians.

_____

_____

☐ Second Check: Did you put a *colon* after the greeting?

> **RULE: When you write a business letter, be sure to *explain* everything *clearly*. Give all the facts the other person needs to know. Don't give unnecessary facts.**

2. Sylvester Lopaka is writing to Acme Rocket Lines. He wants to know about travel to Pluto. Write the *body* of his business letter. Use these facts:

Sylvester has to leave for Pluto on March 1. He wants to stop on Mars for one day. He will have one other person traveling with him. They want to know how much it costs to fly both ways.

Write It   Pretend you want to apply to Ranger School. Write a business letter to the school asking for information.

Try It

Student Rangers often explore new planets. They have to write about the strange things and beings they find. Bonnie wrote about this animal she spotted on the planet Oryx.

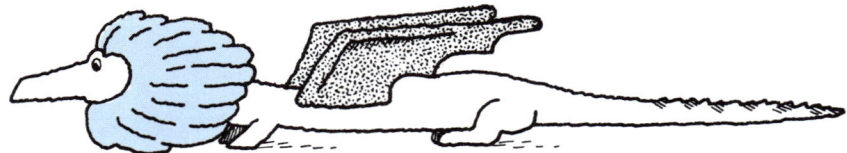

This animal is the size of a cat, about half a meter long. It has a long, thin body and long legs. Its fur is light brown. It has a mane around its neck. Its wings do not have feathers.

Which detail in the report does not describe the animal in the picture?

_____

☐ First Check: Did you choose the *detail* that says the animal has *long legs*?

RULE: When you describe something, look carefully at the object. Use *details* to help you describe.

Bonnie swam underwater in Oryx's ocean. She found some interesting beings. Look at the pictures. Write details about each being.

1.    2.

1. _____

_____

2. _____

_____

3. The people on Oryx travel though the air on special flying chairs. One of the chairs is shown here. Here is a list of details. Put a check next to the ones that fit the picture.

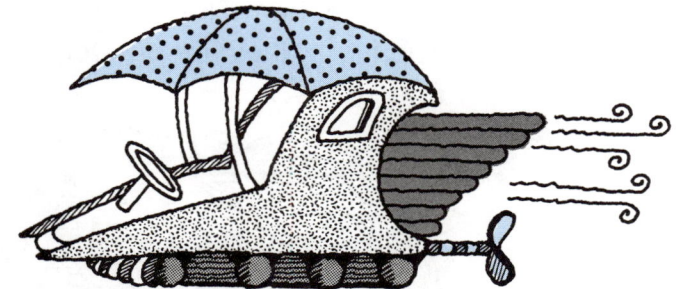

___ There is an umbrella to keep off the sun and rain.
___ The umbrella is connected to the steering wheel.
___ The wings are on either side of the chair's seat.
___ The chair has wheels for ground travel.
___ The propeller is on the back of the chair.
___ The chair has two windows.
___ The chair has a steering wheel.
___ Ten people can sit on the chair.

Use It

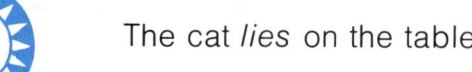

The verbs *lie* and *lay* are often confused. *To lie* means *to stretch oneself out flat*.

    The cat *lies* on the table.

To lay means to *place something down*.

    Brad *lays* the book next to the cat.

Complete each sentence. Write *lie* or *lay* on the lines.

4. Please ___ the maps of Oryx on the table.
5. I will ___ on the couch and study them.
6. The cats like to ___ under the lamp.
7. Do not ___ the code book where the cats can find it.
8. Please ___ the code key next to the book.
9. I think I will ___ here and study the code all night.

4. _____ 6. _____ 8. _____

5. _____ 7. _____ 9. _____

Write It
Write a description of the flying chair in this lesson. In your paragraph use the details you checked in number 3.

Bonnie has to track spaceships at the Einstein City Rocket Port. To do this, she must be able to tell the difference between ships from different planets. Look at the two ships. Ship A is a Martian ship. Ship B is from Pluto. Think about how the two ships are alike. Think about how they are different. Think about things such as *color, size* and *shape*.

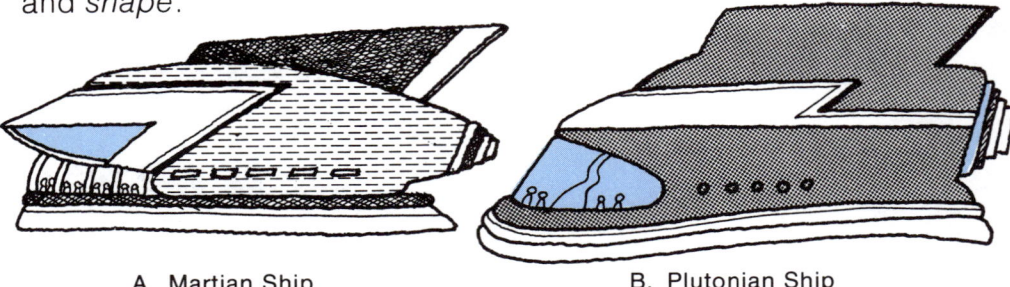

A. Martian Ship   B. Plutonian Ship

1. *Compare* these two ships in a short paragraph. Use the pictures to help you. Tell how the ships are *alike* and how they are *different*.

_____

_____

_____

_____

_____

_____

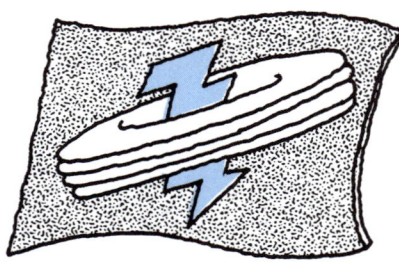
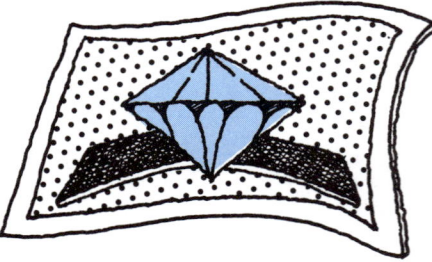

A. Flag of Saturn   B. Flag of Oryx

2. Some spaceships look very much alike. Bonnie has learned to tell them apart by the flags painted on the ships. Here are two flags. Write a short paragraph comparing the two flags. Tell how they are alike and how they are different.

_____

_____

_____

_____

3. Scientists on the moon study animals and plants from many planets. Sometimes the scientists describe the new animals and plants. These two animals come from Oryx. How are they alike? How are they different? Write a short paragraph that compares them.

Animal A

Animal B

_____

_____

_____

_____

_____

_____

USE THE DICTIONARY

A *dictionary entry* shows you how a word should sound. Many letters, especially vowel letters, have special marks over them. Short vowel sounds are usually shown by no mark at all. Sometimes the short vowel sound has the mark: hăt = hat.
Long vowel sounds are shown this way: ā, ē. hāt = hate

(L 46)

1. Angie Vance is going to Rune, where it is always −40° C. She must order an ice suit. Fill out her order form. Use only the details the form asks for.

   Angie is 1.5 m (5 ft.) tall. She weighs 45 kg (99 lbs.). She lives in Room 34, 3 Venus Avenue, Einstein City, Moon. Her ZIP code is M6430. Her favorite color is green. Her shoe size is 6B.

Name _____   **Shoe Size** _____
        FIRST   LAST

Address _____   **Height** _____
        NUMBER & STREET

_____
CITY   STATE OR PLANET   ZIP

Please send 1 ice suit (check one):

☐ **for temperature above 0° C**   ☐ **for temperature 0° C and below**

(L 47)

2. Angie must get from the sleeping quarters to the training center. Here is a map of Einstein City.

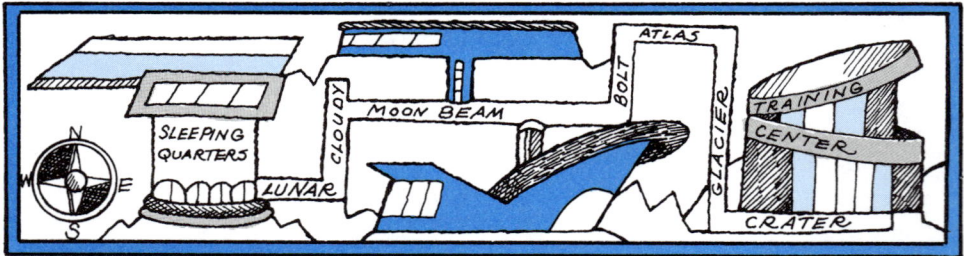

   Complete these directions. Tell how to get from Angie's room to the training center.

   _____

   _____

(L 49)

3. The Chief Space Explorer has sent Angie a business letter. In the letter, he tells Angie to leave the moon on July 19. She must be on Rune by August 12. Angie will be met on Rune by Captain Miron of the Rune Rangers. The Chief Explorer's return address is 78 Pathfinder Street, Earhart City, Venus X7943. His name is Kijuro Tanaka. Angie's address is on page 106. The date of the letter is June 1, 1999. Use this information to write the letter to Angie.

_____

_____

_____

_____

_____

_____

_____

_____

_____

_____

_____

_____

_____

_____

_____

(L 51) 4. Write three sentences that compare the aircar with the moon buggy.

A. Aircar   B. Moon Buggy

_____

_____

_____

Try It

Norma Flagstad is a junior reporter on the Clifftown *Herald*. When she covers a story, she takes *notes*. Usually she must write her notes quickly. Look at these two sets of notes. They were both written in the same amount of time. Which would be more useful for writing a report? Put a check next to the notes you choose.

_____Famous child star, Kip Winston, is making a new movie. "I hope you like it," said Kip. "It will be set in this town . . ."

_____Child star Kip Winston's movie: *The Iron Birds*
Setting: Clifftown near Long River
He stars as Mitchell Breen.
His first movie in a year.

☐   First Check: Did you choose the notes on the *right*?

RULE: Notes are a clear, quick way of writing down information. You can take notes on what someone is saying, or on what you read in a book. When you take notes, write down only the most important details. You can use abbreviations, numerals, and incomplete sentences.

1. Write *notes* about what Kip said. Do not use more than two lines for your notes.

"I was born in Alaska. My birthday is March 1. My parents tell me that it was the coldest March on record. When I was four years old, I was in my first play. It was at Easter, I remember. I had the strangest rabbit suit to wear. It was two sizes too big, and green. Did you ever hear of a green rabbit? Well, I was one."

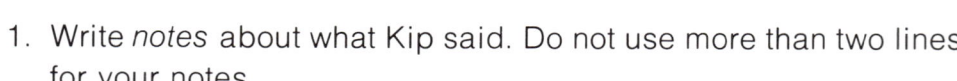

_____

2. Write notes for this paragraph.

   "I was in my first movie when I was six years old. Let me see, was that 1989? No, it was 1988. I remember now. The name of it was *Marnie Flies for a Living*. I played the part of a tightrope walker in a circus family."

   _____

   _____

3. Here are some more notes Norma took on what Kip said. Write a short paragraph from these notes. Write complete sentences.

   1993—acted in movie: *Where Is Meg?* His part: Meg's brother Lou, who searches for her. Was his favorite movie; made in Alaska. Loves that state.

   _____

   _____

   _____

   _____

   _____

☐ Second Check: Did you indent the first sentence of your paragraph?

Write It

Think of something else Kip might say to a reporter. Perhaps he would tell about another film he made or what he does for fun. Write a paragraph that tells what he would say. Think of details he might use in his speech.

Next take notes on your paragraph. Remember, you do not have to use complete sentences.

_____

_____

Try It

Before Norma writes, she arranges her information in *outline form*. This makes the information easier to read and understand. Here is part of an outline for a story on the circus that is coming to Clifftown. Finish Norma's outline by putting the words from the list under the right headings.

List:
Tightrope walking
Trained elephants
Trapeze flying

I.   Animal acts
    A. Tricks by big cats (lions, etc.)
    B. Bareback riding

    C. _____

II. Acts without animals
    A. Clowns

    B. _____

    C. _____

☐   First Check: Did you put *Trained elephants* under the *Animal acts* heading? Did you put the other two acts under the second heading?

RULE: **An *outline* provides a way of grouping information. Outlines are divided into groups and subgroups. The main groups are shown with Roman numerals (I, II, III, IV, V, and so on). Subgroups are shown by capital letters.**

Put this information into *outline form*.

Circuses can be big or small. Small circuses may have only a few animal acts, some high-wire acts, and some clowns. A big circus can have dozens of acts. There are, of course, the usual acts. Often there is also a parade with floats and dancers.

I.   Small circuses: few acts

    A. _____

    B. _____

    C. _____

II. Big circuses: dozens of acts

    A. _____

    B. _____
      1. Floats

      2. _____

Fix It There are several mistakes in this outline. Rewrite the outline in the correct style.

    A. Jumbo the Elephant
      I. Famous circus people
    B. Gargantua the Ape
    A. Emmet Kelly, clown
    B. Clyde Beatty, lion tamer
      II. Famous circus animals

      _____

    A. _____

    B. _____

II. _____

    A. _____

    B. _____

Write It Norma talked to a circus performer. Here are some of Norma's notes. Put the notes into *outline* form.

Much planning before circus: Performers practice; new acts made up.

Other workers: Put up ads, buy food for animals and people, set up tent.

Try It

Paul Murphy is another junior reporter for the *Herald*. Right now he is interviewing Elena Orantes. Elena drives a truck. Here are some of Elena's answers to Paul's questions.

> I live in Clifftown.
> I drive a truck because I enjoy it, and I do it well.
> I started driving trucks three years ago.

What three questions did Paul ask to get those answers? Finish the questions by writing the missing word at the beginning of each question.

_____ do you live?

_____ do you drive a truck?

_____ did you start driving trucks?

☐ First Check: Did you write *Where* for the first question, *Why* for the second question, and *When* for the third?

RULE: Some questions cannot be answered with *yes* or *no*. These questions often begin with the words *who*, *what*, *when*, *where*, *why*, or *how*.

Who is the best driver you know? Ruth is the best driver I know.

Write *questions* for each of the following answers.

1. _____

   My aunt taught me how to drive.

2. _____

   I learned to drive a car when I was 16.

3. _____

   I drive all across the United States.

4. _____

The biggest truck I ever drove was 15 meters (50 feet) long.

5. _____

Trucks can have as many as 18 wheels.

Use It You can make some adjectives show the superlative by adding *est*, as in *biggest* and *smallest*. Other adjectives do not add *est* in the superlative form. With these adjectives, you must use the word *most*. Usually, longer words use *most* instead of *est*. Never use *most* and *est* together.

Wrong: Today is the *most happiest* day of my life.
Right: Today is the *happiest* day of my life.

Write the correct *superlative* form of each underlined adjective.
6. The <u>most importantest</u> drive I ever made was to Maine.
7. I had a load of the <u>most biggest</u> melons you ever saw.
8. The <u>most fastest</u> time I made was 64 km (40 miles) per hour.
9. I saw some of the <u>beautifullest</u> countryside in the United States.

6. _____   8. _____

7. _____   9. _____

Write It Some questions cannot be answered with yes or no. Here is a set of questions that Paul sent to his classmates. What answers would you give to his questions? Your answers should be complete sentences.
10. What job would you most like to have?

_____

11. Why would you like this job?

_____

12. How would you learn about this job?

_____

Try It

Norma is writing a story about the Olympics. Here are three sentences she will use in her story:

A. The modern Olympics began in 1896.
B. The Winter Olympics are more exciting than the Summer Olympics.
C. Everyone should watch the Olympics.

Which sentence above states a *fact*? _____

☐ First Check: Did you say that sentence *A* states a fact?

> **RULE:** **A *fact* is something that can be proved or measured. An *opinion* is a feeling or a belief. An opinion cannot be proved or measured. Sometimes an opinion contains a clue word such as *best, exciting, fun, should, too, beautiful, hate*, or *unfair*.**
>
> *Fact*: The Olympic Games are held in a different place every four years.
> *Opinion*: The Olympics should always be held in the same place.

Look at the sentences. Write *F* in front of each fact. Write *O* in front of each opinion.

_____ 1. The 1896 Olympics were held in Athens, Greece.
_____ 2. Only 12 countries took part.
_____ 3. Now over 100 countries send players to the Games.
_____ 4. The Games should only be held in big cities.
_____ 5. Some sports are no longer part of the Olympics.
_____ 6. New Olympic sports are still being added.
_____ 7. It is too bad that tennis is no longer an Olympic sport.
_____ 8. Roller-skating should be allowed in the Games.
_____ 9. Athletes can win gold, silver, or bronze medals.
_____ 10. The bronze medal is the prettiest medal.

Here is part of Norma's story. Find the *opinions*. Underline each opinion.

11. Women swimmers first entered the Games in 1924. The first women's running events were held in 1928. Women should have all the events men have. It is unfair that there is no

women's marathon or women's weightlifting. Many people are now working to get such events into the Olympics. It will be good if they succeed.

☐ Second Check: Did you find *three opinions*?

Underline each *opinion* in this paragraph.

12. Track and field events make up a large part of the Summer Games. These events include running, jumping, and throwing. The 100-meter dash, the shotput, and the high jump are kinds of track and field events. The jumping events are the most fun to watch. Track and field events aren't as exciting as swimming or diving.

Write It

Write two sentences based on each piece of information. One sentence should state a *fact*. The other should show an *opinion*. Write *F* in front of your fact and *O* in front of your opinion. You do not have to use all the information in your sentences. The first one has been done for you.

> Japan is the only Asian country in which the Olympics have been held. They were held there once.
> Some European countries Olympics have been held in are England, Belgium, Finland, Sweden, Italy, and Austria.

F: There have been many more Olympics in Europe than in Asia.
O: More games should be held in Asia.

13. Some famous American Olympic winners: Babe Didrikson, Jesse Owens, Peggy Fleming, Jim Thorpe, Bob Mathias, Mark Spitz.

F: _____

O: _____

14. Youngest Olympic winner: Marjorie Gestring, 13 years old (diving). Oldest: Oscar Swahn, 72 years old (rifle shooting).

F: _____

O: _____

Try It

Paul wrote this news report for the *Herald*.

> Clifftown's yearly pet show was held in Town Hall yesterday. Pets of all colors, sizes, and shapes were at the show. The biggest pet was Mrs. Harriet Ming's pony, Faust. Faust didn't like the noise. He kicked hard at the wooden slats of his pen. When he kicked, . . .

What happened next? Put a check next to the most likely event.

____ every animal immediately became silent.
____ the slats broke.
____ the show was over.

☐   First Check: Did you choose the *second phrase*?

RULE: Often *one event causes another event to happen.* The first event must happen before the second one can happen.

Choose the *correct ending* for each set of events. Put a check next to the most likely ending.

1. Mrs. Ming and her family fixed Faust's pen. Faust didn't seem any happier about the noise. He tried to kick the pen open again. The Mings knew that music would calm Faust. After Henry Ming brought in a radio and turned it on, . . .

____ Faust got even more excited.
____ Faust was calm.
____ Faust galloped home.

2. Next to Faust was a pen with three gray cats. These cats belonged to Abraham Waupockick of 127 Clark Street. The cats have a special trick. Whenever music plays, they join paws and circle slowly. When Henry played the radio for Faust, . . .

____ the cats kicked at their pen.
____ the cats joined paws and circled to the music.
____ the cats sang a short song.

3. Every year a prize for the best-looking dog is given. No dog is ever given the prize two years in a row. Last year Clara Bock's Irish setter, Tex, won the prize. This year the two most beautiful dogs were Tex and Ahmed Halevi's greyhound, Arrow. When the judge announced her decision, . . .

___ Tex was the winner.
___ Arrow was the winner.
___ There was no winner.

Use It

The verbs *bring* and *take* both mean *to carry*. But they are used at different times. The verb *bring* means *to come carrying* something. *Take* means *to go carrying* something. One way to remember this is, "Bring here, take there."

Bring the canary to me.   *Take* the birds to those cages.

Finish each sentence. Write *bring* or *take* on the lines.

4. Craig will ___ the next group of animals over here to be judged.
5. Please ___ the chairs away to that corner.
6. Will the owners of all mice, goldfish, and rabbits please ___ their pets to me?
7. Do not ___ any cats over here.
8. The biggest rabbit will ___ away the prize when it leaves.
9. Please ___ my rabbit's collar to me.

4. _____   6. _____   8. _____

5. _____   7. _____   9. _____

Write It

Read about these events. Write a sentence that tells what you think happened next.

10. Then all the cats were put on a long table to be judged. Portia and The Beast, who always fight, were accidentally put next to each other. Because they were so close to each other, . . .

_____

_____

11. After that the birds were brought out. Each bird owner was told to hold on to his or her bird. The judges didn't want the birds to get loose. Hannah Ellu was holding her canary, Ruggles. When Hannah sneezed, . . . _____

_____

A *news story* must give *facts clearly*. It should also give facts in an interesting way. Look at this news story.

(DPI) On Friday, October 13, people living on Rivera Avenue saw a strange object in the sky over their houses. The round object was at first thought to be a spaceship. Several people said they saw lights blinking on and off in the object.

Look at the first sentence of the story. The beginning of a news story should answer the questions *who, what, when*, and *where*. Sometimes the questions *why* and *how* are also answered. How does the news story answer these questions? Answer each *wh* question.

1. Who? _____

2. What? _____

3. When? _____

4. Where? _____

5. Write the first few sentences of a news story. Choose one thing from each list for your story.

Who	What	When	Where
Margo Gutman, a bookkeeper	won a long distance bicycle race	yesterday	in the nearby woods
Fritz Schrodinger, a teacher	caught a runaway cub from the zoo	at 5:34 P.M. last Monday	at Palm Valley, 25 kilometers away
Lee Ann Jones, a 10-year-old girl	saw what might have been a wizard on a flying carpet	earlier this week	here in town

_____

_____

_____

_____

118

6. A news writer should know the difference between *facts* and *opinions*. News reporters should never state opinions as if they were facts. Here are some statements about the unknown object seen in the sky over Rivera Avenue. Put an *F* in front of each fact. Then use all of the facts to write the end of the story about the UFO. Add three more facts to the story.

_____ The object floated about 30 meters (100 feet) high.
_____ It was the scariest thing anyone had ever seen.
_____ It turned out to be a big balloon invented by Cyrus Hooper.
_____ Mr. Hooper was enjoying a night flight in his balloon.
_____ The blinking lights were his air-powered lighting system.
_____ Balloons should not be allowed to fly at night.

_____

_____

_____

_____

_____

_____

_____

_____

USE THE DICTIONARY

You will often find the *schwa* (ə) in a dictionary entry. The schwa stands for a "swallowed vowel sound." It is the *a* sound in *about*, the *e* in *happen*, the *i* in *edible*, the *o* in *gallop*, and the *u* in *circus*.

Circle the schwa sound in each of these words.

ago	even	adore	period
around	Venus	again	fallen
human	bitten	alike	chorus

59 Review

(L 53)   1. Take notes on this paragraph. Write your notes on the lines.

       Clifftown School has a mystery. For the last three weeks, there have been strange noises in the early morning. At night other odd things have been happening. Last Monday all the chairs in the fourth-grade classroom were under the desks. That same day all the chalk in the sixth grade floated in the air. The students think it's a ghost.

_____

_____

_____

(L 54)   2. Complete the outline using this information

       There have been two kinds of strange events in Clifftown School. The first is strange sounds. These include slamming doors and laughter. Odd sights include shiny red balls flying through the air and furniture moving by itself.

   I.   Sounds

      A. _____

      B. _____

   II. _____

      A. _____

      B. _____

(L 55)   Use the information on this page to answer these questions. Use complete sentences in your answers.

   3. Where are the strange events taking place?

_____

   4. What things are happening?

_____

120

5. When were the chairs found under the desk ?

_____

6. Why might all this be happening?

_____

(L 56) Which statements are facts? Write *F* next to each fact. Write *O* next to each opinion.

_____ 7. The school was once a family's home.
_____ 8. The owner's name was Winthrop Massingill.
_____ 9. I'm sure Winthrop Massingill is the ghost.
_____ 10. You're silly if you think he is the ghost.
_____ 11. A picture of Winthrop Massingill is in one classroom.

(L 56) 12. Use this information to write two sentences. The first sentence should state a fact. The second should show an opinion.

The students who saw things moving: 23 fifth graders, 21 sixth graders, a fourth grader, and the entire kindergarten.

Fact: _____

Opinion: _____

(L 57) Look at this paragraph. What is the event most likely to happen next? Check that event.

One night groups of students and teachers hid themselves in the school. Andrea Fast and Mrs. Habib hid in the fifth-grade classroom. They could see Winthrop Massingill's picture from where they hid. Suddenly, a strange light started to come from the picture. The light moved a little. Then the picture seemed to come alive. Since the man in the picture was Winthrop Massingill,

____ a. there was no ghost in the school.
____ b. Andrea and Mrs. Habib should not have hid in the room.
____ c. perhaps people had seen the ghost of Mr. Massingill.

(L 46) Clifftown is starting a theater school. Joan has applied to the school. Use this information to fill out the *form*.

1. Joan is 12 years old. She lives on Magnus Street. She is 1.4m (4 ft. 9 in.) tall and weighs 34 kg (75 lbs.). Her house number is 43. She lives in Clifftown, North Dakota. Her ZIP code is 58746. Joan's last name is Kimura. She has acted in school plays. Her middle name is Nobu.

Name _____

       FIRST   MIDDLE   LAST

Address _____

      HOUSE NUMBER AND STREET

_____

      CITY   STATE   ZIP

Have you ever acted before? ☐ **yes**   ☐ **no**

(L 47) 2. The map shows part of Clifftown. How will Joan walk to the theater? Write the first two steps of her trip.

_____

_____

(L 50) 3. Joan's picture is next to the map. Write a description of what Joan is wearing. Include at least two details.

_____

_____

(L 53) 4. Take *notes* on what the teacher said in Joan's theater class.

"Good morning class. Welcome to theater school. The first play we will do is *The Fallen Mountain*. There are three leading characters: Sabrina, Augustus, and Dr. Waldorf. The play takes place in the year 1887. It is set in Vermont."

_____

_____

(L 54) 5. Use the same information to complete this *outline*.

    I. Characters

        A. _____

        B. _____

        C. _____

   II. Story

        A. Time: _____

        B. Place: _____

(L 55) Write the *questions* for these answers.

6. _____

The names of the main characters are Sabrina, Augustus, and Dr. Waldorf.

7. _____

We will put on the play on Monday, November 7.

8. _____

Joan will play the part of Sabrina.

9. _____

The play takes place near a state forest.

(L 56) Underline each *fact*.

10. This play is the best play Mark Creighton ever wrote.
11. It was written in 1921.
12. It should always be played on an outdoor stage.

Glossary of Rules

ABBREVIATIONS: An abbreviation is a shortened form of a word. Words are abbreviated because they are used regularly. Most abbreviations end with periods. The names of groups and organizations usually have more than one word in them. These names can be abbreviated by using the first letter of each word. Small words like *and, of,* and *the* are not usually included in the abbreviation. (Lesson 3)

ADJECTIVES: Adjectives are descriptive words. They are words that describe, picture, or tell more about people, places, or things. More than one adjective can be used with a single noun. (Lesson 16) When adjectives are used to compare two people or things, the endings *er* and *est* are added. Add *er* when comparing two people or things. Add *est* when comparing more than two people or things. (Lesson 17) The words *more* and *most* are used with adjectives to compare people and things. Use *more* to compare two people or things. Use *most* to compare more than two people or things. *More* and *most* are usually used with adjectives that have three or more syllables. (Lesson 18)

ADVERBS: Adverbs are descriptive words. Adverbs work with verbs by telling how, when, or where an action occurs. Adverbs often end in *ly*. Adverbs can often be formed by adding *ly* to an adjective. The final *y* of an adjective changes to *i* before adding *ly*. (Lesson 19) A group of words can act as an adverb. (Lesson 20) You can often combine sentences by using more than one adverb. (Lesson 27)

APOSTROPHES: To write the possessive of a singular noun add an apostrophe (') and *s.* Add only an apostrophe to plural nouns and other nouns that end in *s.* (Lesson 5) A contraction is a shortened form of one or two words. Many contractions are formed with a pronoun and a helping verb. An apostrophe shows where one or more letters have been left out. (Lesson 12)

APPLICATIONS: Read applications and other forms carefully. Fill in all the necessary information. Check to see whether your last name should be written first. (Lesson 46)

CAPITALIZATION: Proper nouns begin with capital letters. Titles of books, magazines, and movies are capitalized. Begin each word in a title with a capital letter, except for small words such as *in, or, by, to, the,*

124

and, with, and *of.* The first word of a title is always written with a capital letter. (Lesson 2) In a quotation, the speaker's first word begins with a capital letter. (Lesson 33)

CLAUSES: A clause is a word group within a sentence. A clause has its own subject and verb. Many clauses begin with the words *before, since, after, while, if, where, because,* or *although.* These clauses cannot stand alone as complete sentences. (Lesson 40)

COMMAS: Use a comma to separate each word or group of words listed in a series. Do not use a comma after the last word in a series. (Lesson 31) When writing a date that includes the year, place a comma between the day and the year. If the date does not end the sentence, place a comma after the year, too. When writing the name of a city and state, place a comma between the name of the city and state. If the name of the state does not end the sentence, place a comma after the state. When a sentence starts with an introductory word, or a person's name, there is a pause or short stop after that word. A comma should be written after the word to show the pause. If a sentence ends with the name of a person being spoken to, place a comma before the name. (Lesson 32) A dialogue tag tells who is speaking. Use a comma to separate the dialogue tag from the words being spoken. (Lesson 33)

CONTRACTIONS: A contraction is a shortened form of a word or words. Many contractions are formed with a pronoun and helping verb. An apostrophe shows where one or more letters have been left out. A negative contraction is formed when a helping verb is combined with the word *not.* (Lesson 12)

DIRECTIONS: When writing directions, write all the steps in order. Do not leave out any steps. (Lesson 47)

INVITATIONS: An invitation should tell the kind of event, the date and time, and the place. (Lesson 48)

LETTERS: A friendly letter has five parts: the heading, the greeting, the body, the closing, and the signature. (Lesson 34) A business letter has a sixth part—the inside address. The greeting of a business letter is followed by a colon. (Lesson 49)

NOUNS: Nouns name people, animals, places, or things. A singular noun names one person, animal, place, or thing. A plural noun names more than one. Add *s* to most nouns to make them plural. Add *es* to singular nouns that end in *s, x, ch,* or *sh.* Some words have irregular plural forms. The spelling of these words change when they become plural. (Lesson 1) Words that name classes of people, places, and things are common nouns. Words that name specific people, places, or things are proper nouns. Proper nouns begin with capital letters. (Lesson 2) The names of groups and organizations are proper nouns. These proper nouns often have more than one word in them. (Lesson 3) Nouns can show ownership or possession. To write the possessive form of a singular noun add an apostrophe and *s.* Add only an apostrophe to plural nouns and other nouns that end is *s.* (Lesson 5)

OUTLINES: An outline provides a way to organize information. Outlines divide information into main groups and subgroups. The main groups are shown with Roman numerals. (Lesson 54)

PARAGRAPHS: In written conversation, a new paragraph begins each time the speaker changes. (Lesson 33) A paragraph is a group of sentences about the same subject. The sentences in a paragraph should follow each other in some kind of order. The order in which things happen in time is one kind of order. (Lesson 41)

PHRASES: A phrase is a group of words that goes together. A phrase does not have a subject or a verb. All the words in a phrase have the same purpose. They tell when, where, how, what kind, or to whom. Adjectives phrases describe people, places, or things. (Lesson 39)

PREDICATES: The simple predicate is the verb that tells what the subject *is* or *does*. The complete predicate of a sentence tells more about the simple predicate. (Lesson 24) Some sentences have a compound predicate. A compound predicate is two verbs. It tells two different things that a subject of a sentence does. (Lesson 25)

PRONOUNS: A pronoun can be used in place of a noun. *I, you, he, she, it, we,* and *they* are subject pronouns. These pronouns tell who or what does something in a sentence. The object pronouns are *me, you,*

126

him, her, it, us, and *them.* These pronouns usually come after a verb or a preposition in a sentence. (Lesson 4) Some pronouns show ownership. They are called possessive pronouns. (Lesson 5)

QUOTATIONS: The exact words of a speaker are a quotation and should be enclosed in quotation marks. (Lesson 33) When a quotation ends a sentence, the period, question mark, or exclamation point is written inside the quotation mark. (Lesson 35)

SENTENCES: A sentence that tells something is called a statement. A statement ends with a period. A sentence that asks is a question. A question ends with question mark. A sentence that shows strong feeling ends with an exclamation point. This type of sentence is called an exclamation. (Lesson 23) There are many ways to combine sentences. You can combine sentences by using more than one adjective. You can combine similar sentences that have groups of words that tell where, when, or how. (Lesson 27)

SENTENCE AGREEMENT: The subject and predicate of a sentence must agree. A singular subject takes the singular form of the verb in the predicate. A plural subject takes the plural form of the verb. (Lesson 26) Use the plural form of the verb in sentences with compound subjects. (Lesson 26)

SERIES: A list of three or more words or groups of words in a sentence is a series. Use a comma to separate each word or group of words listed in a series. Do not use a comma after the last word in a series. (Lesson 31)

SUBJECTS: The simple subject of a sentence is a noun or pronoun that tells *who* or *what* does something. The simple subject is what the sentence is about. The complete subject of a sentence is all the words that make up the subject part of the sentence. The complete subject tells more about the simple subject. (Lesson 24) Some sentences have a compound subject. A compound subject is two subjects joined by the word *and* or *or*. (Lesson 25)

VERBS: A verb is a word that shows action or being. A verb shows time through its different forms. The present tense tells what is happening now. It also shows what happens regularly. The past tense of a verb tells what happened in the past. The past tense is often formed by adding *ed* to the present tense. The future tense of a verb tells what will happen in the future. It is formed by using the word *will* before the present tense of the verb. (Lesson 8) The past tense of many verbs is not formed by adding *d* or *ed*. Irregular verbs change their spelling in the past tense. Often only one vowel in the word changes. (Lesson 9) The verbs *be* and *have* have many forms. Use *is* or *was* when you talk about only one. Use *are* or *were* when you talk about more than one. Use *am* and *was* when you talk about yourself. Use *are* and *were* with the word *you*. Use *has* when you talk about one. Use *have* when you talk about more than one. Use *had* when you talk about the past. (Lesson 10) A verb that is used with the main verb is called a helping verb. A main verb can have more than one helping verb. The helping verbs and the main verb make up a verb phrase. The last verb in the phrase is the main verb. (Lesson 11)